Crossing the Wire

Crossing the Wire

*One Woman's Journey
into the Hidden Dangers
of the Afghan War*

AnnaMaria Cardinalli, Ph.D.

CASEMATE

Philadelphia & Oxford

Published in the United States of America and Great Britain in 2013 by
CASEMATE PUBLISHERS
908 Darby Road, Havertown, PA 19083
and
10 Hythe Bridge Street, Oxford, OX1 2EW

ISBN 978-1-61200-191-3
Digital Edition: ISBN 978-1-61200-201-9

Cataloging-in-publication data is available from the Library of Congress
and the British Library.

10 9 8 7 6 5 4 3 2 1

Printed and bound in the United States of America.

All images used in this book have been credited where possible. The publisher
will gladly make corrections to attribution in subsequent printings of the book.

For a complete list of Casemate titles please contact:

CASEMATE PUBLISHERS (US)
Telephone (610) 853-9131, Fax (610) 853-9146
E-mail: casemate@casematepublishing.com

CASEMATE PUBLISHERS (UK)
Telephone (01865) 241249, Fax (01865) 794449
E-mail: casemate-uk@casematepublishing.co.uk

Contents

	Introduction	9
	Prologue	13
1	C-130 Rolling Down the Strip	15
2	Mamma Told Me Not to Come!	33
3	In the Clutches of the Mullah	39
4	Bow-Wow, Kuchi Coup	51
5	"So, What's a Nice Girl Like You Doing in a Place Like This?"	57
6	Villages Without Medicines: Stomachs First	75
7	Latrines and Shower Scenes	79
8	Huh? What Does It Mean?	93
9	Boots Don't Bend	104
10	" . . . Too Damn Cruel"	106
11	"If They Are Stronger, It Is Theirs for Them to Take."	111
12	We Spell Misery M.R.E.	123
13	Playing I.E.D. Chicken	127
14	To Walk a Mile for a Camel	131
15	"If You Go to a Medic, You Had Better be Missing a Limb."	136
16	Really? No, Really?	139
17	Incoming!	155
18	The First U.S.M.C. Female Engagement Team	161
19	NATO Soldiers as Objects	179
20	It Doesn't End There	200
21	Afghanistan, Againistan	211
22	Farewell to Foreign Shores . . .	219
23	In From the Cold	227
	Epilogue	234
	Notes	239

To those who serve,
and to the innocent they protect.

And to my Mom, Giovanna Cardinalli, in so many ways the bravest of all.

Before Proceeding

A book of this nature requires a few important disclaimers. First, the entire text of this manuscript is unclassified and has been subject to a classification review by U.S. Government authorities.

Second, I am writing simply as a private individual, sharing my personal experiences and memories of war. I am not acting as an employee of or in any official capacity for the U.S. Army Human Terrain System, or for any of the services or agencies with which I have worked. My views and analyses are simply my own.

Third, this book does not generally convey the intent of my specific missions or findings for the Human Terrain System, the United States Marine Corps, the United States Army, or British forces, because these were frequently of operational relevance. While Human Terrain findings are unclassified, I see no reason to unnecessarily publicize sensitive information when it can potentially involve the protection of American and Afghan lives.

Finally, this book would not have been published without the shared convictions of David Farnsworth at Casemate, his editor Steven Smith, and the generous staff there, as well as Jane Friedman, Tina Pohlman, and the professional eBook publishing team at Open Road Media. For the manuscript to arrive in their hands, my agents Peter and Sandra Riva, along with JoAnn Collins, never wavered in their understanding of the import of the tale I had to tell. All these deserve my thanks and appreciation.

Introduction

"Crossing the wire" is a phrase that carries deep meaning in the heart of anyone who has fought in a counterinsurgency effort, like that of our long War on Terror. It means a venture past the ambiguous front line and into the chaotic uncertainty of warfare. It is beyond the wire where battle lies. Paradoxically, it is only by crossing the wire that the human complexities that create and underlie conflict become apparent, and it is only in the effort to reveal and untangle them that lie our long-term chances for victory, resolution, and peace.

The venture across the wire is one that only a small number even among our military ever make, and impossibly few among them are women. A strange life journey ultimately placed me—a woman, an opera singer and classical guitarist by profession, a Catholic theologian by education, and an intelligence professional by fierce patriotism—outside the wire in Afghanistan and found me tasked, among many things, with an investigation of the issue of sexuality in the remote Pashtun south of the country, the region from which a great part of the terrorist threat to the Western world originates and is nurtured and harbored. Incredibly, I found the issue of sex to be central to that incubation of violence.

My official government report on the subject for the U.S. Army Human Terrain System, originally intended for a limited military and academic readership, was termed "explosive" and leaked into mainstream American media, where it generated a firestorm of reaction in a variety of major national news outlets. Some of my findings regarding Afghan sexual practices were simply of sociological interest, such as the prevalence of culturally and environmentally influenced homosexual behaviors among men. Other findings, however, were of grave humanitarian concern, such as the cyclical abuse of young boys, perpetuated over countless generations. Because the topic became intensely sensationalized, I was discouraged to see my findings somewhat distorted in the public light—their real meaning often lost in the shock value of the subject and occasionally manipulated to make points that I believed unfounded.

In this book, I take the opportunity to provide the full context of my research in the hope of offering readers a more complete background through which to both understand the reasons for my conclusions and to draw their own. Instead of presenting a further academic account, I here invite you to share personally in the daily experiences and challenges of a woman living and patrolling on the farthest front of the War on Terror, and to witness with me the sometimes surreal difficulties faced and heartening heroism displayed by the men and women—Coalition and Afghan —whose lives protect our own. I hope that by walking with me, you come to experience the ways in which the issue of Afghan sexuality has profound impact on concerns from women's rights, to Afghanistan's economic development and security, to the recruitment and development of the terrorist threat to the Western world—a threat, I ultimately argue, we will not be free of without attention to this cycle of violence.

In the vein of addressing the human complexities of conflict, I also want to thank you, the reader, as your purchase of this book has already made a real and active difference toward the betterment of individual lives as they directly relate to many of the troublesome concerns this book will address. One portion of the book proceeds will be donated to the Polaris Project (polarispoject.org), one of the largest and most successful efforts in combating human trafficking and child prostitution both internationally and in the U.S. (lest we fail to see and address problems on our own doorstep when we look to identify them elsewhere). A second portion will go to benefit the recovery of heroes in the VA hospital system who bear the typical wounds of our current wars—amputations, head injuries, and severe PTSD—through the Jam for Vets Project (jamforvets.org), which by giving veterans a new voice through music instruction, therapy, and the gift of an instrument, creates a sometimes otherwise inaccessible path to healing and to the restoration of our common humanity (a project after my own heart).

By your interest in learning more about the reality of the Afghan conflict, and your active participation in helping these causes through your purchase, you've already fought a significant part of a battle that affects us all. Although this book will come to some hard conclusions, I find hope in the realization that every bit of good is a necessary footstep toward a greater solution. You have my thanks.

A first encounter.

Prologue

My Mom always told me to keep a diary, and she was right. There is so much we fail to understand and easily forget from each day to the next. But if our memories are preserved over time, sometimes we can later see a picture that we otherwise would never have imagined was there.

What I offer here is, in essence, my diary—the faded and battered notebook I carried through a treacherous war. It is repaired of its tears and tatters. I have written out the meaning of the cryptic notes only I understood. I have put into words the poor sketches that reminded me of a person, or a pivotal conversation, or an experience I could not better describe. I have made some sense of the fragmented thoughts that troubled me when I first wrote them.

I have torn out most pages that described only the mundane experience of a sand-colored life in a sand-colored world, but there were so very many. I have likewise eliminated the misguided love notes, the cheerful letters home, and the prayers which were the only place I dared admit my real fear. What is left is simply the path of my bootprints and my thoughts in the bizarre journey they took.

These are not my "field notes," the academic journals through which I conducted careful and detached analysis for my program and commanders. The result of that work has already been leaked publicly, and it has unfortunately generated more controversy than understanding. It is for that reason that I wish to share my own story—to provide the context in which those findings lay.

They say that a girl is always loath to share her diary, but I offer mine here with the sincere hope that you, the reader, will view the experience of war along with me. By lending you my eyes as I patrolled southern Afghanistan in 2009 as the Senior Social Scientist on a Human Terrain Team (HTT), and sharing with you the unlikely story that led to my participation in this war, I hope that this book makes the issues that arise both more human and concrete.

CHAPTER 1

C-130 Rolling Down
the Strip

● DAY 1

"**C**-one-thirty rolling down the strip. HTT's going to take a little trip."

The silly old song played through my mind, despite my attempts to think of anything more serious.

"Mission Top Secret, destination unknown. We don't know if we're coming home."

As I sat lodged in the belly of the C-130 aircraft, having found my space between some tank components and a slightly more comfortable shipment of tires, I hummed along to the familiar tune. It had been chanted for generations by members of the U.S. military as they shared a morning run. I smiled to think of the tradition and the fact that, somewhat implausibly, I had found myself a participant. Slowly, it occurred to me that the song raised the questions that lay just below the surface of my awareness.

Everybody inserted the name of their own team or unit into the song, but what did it mean to be a member of HTT—a Human Terrain Team? Our team was flying toward the most remote tribal badlands of Afghanistan, the outermost limits of Western presence. We were the only team attached to the U.S. Marine Corps, and I was enormously proud of the fact. Only a few months before, the Marines had just began to secure the dangerous area, which had been considered untamable for countless generations. I had to wonder what, exactly, a gung-ho but utterly "girly" and almost comically diminutive woman was to accomplish there.

The mission was, in its own way, secret even to me. All I truly knew was that our purpose was to protect American and Afghan lives by uncovering hidden cultural differences that could cause unnecessary conflict— as arose tragically in the early phases of the Iraq war—and by identifying the ways Western forces could best assist the Afghan people. We were to do this by venturing beyond the lines where academic involvement typically ends and the work of warfighting typically begins.

Today was not the first time I found myself on a C-130 that would deliver me spiraling into a war zone. As an Intelligence Analyst for the FBI, I had been attached to the Joint Special Operations Command in Iraq. There, I supported the most forward efforts against terrorism with the intent of preventing attacks on U.S. soil.

I wasn't the person who rushed out on daring assignments, however. I was the person who worked out the meaning of what was discovered. My experience of war in Afghanistan is bound to be different, as I am now charged with a highly unusual combination of both.

The U.S. has truly realized that subtle and variable local cultural differences cannot be discovered in a book or from a purported expert. Instead, they have to be learned directly from the Afghan people. This can only be accomplished by putting those charged with investigating these matters up front, at times ahead of the major body of U.S. forces, to learn the nuances of the local culture by interacting with and interviewing the communities themselves. The HTT program hires highly motivated, ideologically driven, and slightly reckless civilian Ph.D.-level researchers, just like me, to lead the studies.

It was also true, in a way, that our destination was unknown. In the academic sense, we can never know in advance where our research might lead us or what unanticipated turns it might take. Neither do we know what our personal fate or that of our team might be.

Being among the first to collect information means that HTT members never know who they might be encountering. On initial meeting, we are warned, one can never quite tell an angry insurgent bent on violence from a friendly and innocent villager, as the former often pose as the latter. This confusion opens a wide door for those who wish to do us harm to approach closely and attack almost unopposed.

This thought weighed on me with unusual poignancy and not a small amount of carefully suppressed terror. Just before deploying, my team and I attended the memorial service of another female HTT researcher—Paula Loyd. I never knew Paula, but I know that her unimaginable bravery and dedication to the assistance of the Afghan people should be remembered always. A "prayer card" from her service was tucked in a corner of my rucksack, and in my Catholic schoolgirl way, I was sure she would be praying for the teams still on the ground.

Paula, of course, was not the only HTT member recently killed in service. For such a small new program, we seem to have seen a disproportionate number of casualties. However, Paula's tale haunted me in an uncomfortable number of ways. The stories I heard about her work seemed to say something troubling about the Afghan communities that I am so enthusiastic to encounter and hopeful to assist.

Paula, as I learned, had been absolutely impossible to deter in her efforts to help the Afghan people—particularly Afghan women—though she often faced the opposition of the very individuals she sought to aid. While some of this opposition was undoubtedly unwitting, some of it seemed troublingly willful. There are iconic stories about Paula's efforts that have circulated to almost legendary proportions.

Friends in the program tell me that when Paula was working for an aid organization before joining HTT, she assisted a village in developing a sustainable (non-narcotic) income source by planting an apricot orchard. Unlike many other fruit trees, these apricot trees would mature and bear a saleable and highly profitable crop in four years—a fantastically reasonable amount of time. In those four years, Paula devoted tireless efforts to both the cultivation of the young and fledgling orchard and to sustaining the village's various other needs.

The women of the village were empowered by assisting in the cultivation. They were helping to build their families' futures. This was one of Paula's most important goals.

As the story goes, Paula visited the U.S. to celebrate Christmas with her family just before the spring of the fourth year. When she returned, she found the orchard cut down and the trees used for firewood. Dismayed, she asked why the just-matured trees had been burned when plenty of fuel had already been provided and sat unused. The response she received from the town's kingpin was, "Yes, there was fuel, but none of it smelled as sweet as the apricot when it burned."

Later, after joining HTT, Paula stopped to visit with a vendor at a small bazaar and discuss the price of kerosene. Engaging with a local resident about a topic like this was a typical daily task for an HTT member. The vendor's warm response and kind smile invited her to continue in conversation.

HTT members seldom miss an opportunity to chat. Simple, friendly conversation is the best means of absorbing cultural nuance. The availability of kerosene was an important and relevant topic in the daily life of a village, and Paula was keen to know more. The remarkably pleasant vendor expressed his appreciation for Paula's interest and invited her closer.

Casually, the vendor picked up a container of his kerosene with the apparent intent, like that of most bazaar vendors, of showing off its quality. The vendor then, in an incredibly deft motion, doused Paula with the liquid and set a flame to her. Her body lit instantaneously. This thought alone sickens me with fear, but Paula's ordeal did not end there.

The vendor ran away, having accidentally set his own hands on fire. A nearby teammate of Paula's, unaware of the circumstances, aided the man by rolling on top of him to extinguish the flames. It was a heroic attempt on his part to show American dedication to protect Afghan lives.

However, Paula's teammate quickly learned the truth of the situation after seeing Paula and witnessing the vendor's prompt arrest by local authorities. Horrified, Paula's teammate shot the attacker, point-blank, in the head. Shooting a detained man was a crime that would change the teammate's life forever, but it ensured the vendor would not enter the undeveloped Afghan justice system, where he, like other terrorists, would be released within a matter of days.

In the meantime, the rest of the team had run to Paula's aid. In a desperate attempt to douse the flames, they threw her into the nearest water source available—the local stream. It, like that of most villages, was heavy with sewage.

Paula wasn't lucky enough to meet a quick death, but one of tortuous endurance over several months. The treatment for full-body burns—consisting of constant "debridement"—is almost barbaric in its brutality. We were updated constantly about her condition throughout our HTT training and told how she handled the pain with all the grace imaginable. She very well might have lived had her body had not become completely infected by the waste-infested water of the village.

Paula's story leaves no room for doubt that this mission is fraught with cruel dangers—not just the flying bullets and bombs that seem typical of war—but those particularly terrorizing acts that can arise from extreme cultural and ideological differences. This time, like the old song says, we don't know if we were coming home. If the information is worth the risk, I can't help but wonder what might be the hidden mysteries of this culture that I am being charged to uncover.

Dawn patrol.

● DAY 2 We have arrived too early. Camp Leatherneck, the planned bastion of the USMC presence in southern Afghanistan from which we are to base our operations, does not quite yet exist. From the C-130, we took a helicopter to the location where Leatherneck should have been. The helicopter let us off, crewmen helpfully tossing our bags out after us, and we charged like commandos just to remain on our feet against the power of the rushing blast generated by the propellers.

In a few seconds, we found ourselves standing alone, each encumbered by four enormous and battered olive-green bags, and surrounded by darkness and silence so complete it seemed limitless. The stench of fuel was the only detail that reminded us where we were. Much like hapless tourists mistakenly dropped off in the "bad" part of town at the worst time of night, we had no idea where to go. Also, far more ominously, we couldn't be sure what might wait for us in the still blackness.

We dragged ourselves and our bags in the direction we deemed to be "forward" until we ran into the fabric wall of a tent. After groping for an entrance and fumbling for the string to a light bulb, we enjoyed an unimaginably welcome sight—food. Someone had left M.R.E.'s for us. It meant that we were where we were supposed to be.

In a few hours, dawn neared, and an earnest young Marine pulled up in a decrepit Pakistani minivan. My sleep-deprived mind settled into a cheerful place thanks to the incongruity of the Marine in his minivan, the newness of the adventure, and the promise of the good we might accomplish ahead. The quickly increasing heat of the rising sun smiled on us as we traveled the dusty miles to where Leatherneck actually began.

I thought warmly of my companions in the minivan. We were a team of four, facing work that would take an army in itself. I did not know them well, but I thought I knew them enough. They had been in my training class, though they were not from the team with which I had originally trained to deploy. Still, I thought we made a perfect combination—two men and two women.

The other woman, an analyst, shared a Hispanic heritage with me, and I thought this might make us close. She hadn't disclosed much about herself, but I noticed she loved a college football team from Texas. No matter the military attire our circumstances might require, she somehow usually managed to fit her Texas football t-shirt into the outfit.

Not knowing her better, in my mind I called her Tex. (Every military story seems to include a friend named "Tex," as I have learned from the movies.) At one time, I learned, she had been a truck driver in the Army. A girl who's hard to mess with, I thought. I liked Tex.

The male analyst I admired for his dedication to his family. He was a bit shorter and rounder than most, but there was something shining about him—and it wasn't his balding pate. I could see his eyes light up every time he spoke of his new baby. I had met the baby, and his wife, at a party our program threw before deploying us. We were all full of good wine and laughing away our fears and tension, but not him. He only had eyes for his family. The definition of a man, I thought. I called him Pop.

The team leader I called Lanky. He was. With his height came a take-charge attitude, and I admired his confidence. He had thick dark hair and glowering eyebrows, which he tended to squeeze together, but this only added to his appearance of authority.

Originally trained as an analyst, Lanky was just recently thrown into his team leader position when someone of higher rank abruptly left the program, and he accepted the challenge proudly. He was the picture of a soldier. I couldn't recall if I had ever seen him out of his Army cammies, and if he said anything often, it was that he knew "how the Army really works." I was pleased with the idea that our team was in such self-assured hands.

I held the program title and rank of Senior Social Scientist, which I found funny as I was most likely the *only* social scientist for hundreds of miles. While Lanky directed our operations militarily, I led our research mission. I fully expected a wonderful symbiosis as we began to work together.

The rising sun was made more beautiful by the haze of red sand that lingered endlessly in the sky. The same sand, however, quickly prompted us all to pull scarves or shawls over our heads, ears, noses, and mouths, in quick order becoming unintentionally but properly dressed to fit in easily with locals. (There's a reason people dress the way they do in the desert. It works.) The windows on the minivan were all broken out or inoperably jammed open, and the faster we traveled, the faster the fine, sharp, and choking sand came at us.

The sand-clogged air, however, was the cleanest that we would breathe. An enormous plume of lazily rising black smoke announced Leatherneck on the horizon. We smelled the camp long before we reached it. The plume was the product of the fact that neither American nor Afghan political will would allow us to install any building projects that gave the impression of intended permanence, such as waste-disposal facilities.

Therefore, everything was burned. The fuel for the flames today was a mixture of smoldering plastic and rubber, machine parts and gasoline, and a heaping contribution of kitchen, bathroom, and medical waste. I was certain that I would never be able to forget the unmistakable acridity of that smell, no matter the time or distance I eventually put between myself and it.

Leatherneck itself was an unimaginably vast series of identical tents and cement blast barriers, their color perfectly matched to the desert that surrounded them and the sand that swirled about them. If not for their shadows, I imagined that one might not be able to see them at all. The camp already housed thousands of Marines in their equally color-matched cammies, and the effect was both stunning and a bit unnerving in its perfect regularity.

After being shown into the tent where I was assigned a bunk, I wondered how I would ever find it again. There was not a single feature that would indicate my tent's difference from the next. I knew no one who might help me back, and in my disorientation, I was struck with an intense if illogical sense of being lost and alone.

I stepped outside my tent into the sun and watched dusty but ever-formal Marines pass me by. "Good morning, ma'am," each would nod po-

Bunks at Leatherneck.
(Photo courtesy
Department of Defense)

litely, not yet quite knowing who I was and a bit disconcerted to find a civilian woman in their midst. Still, in most faces was a determination I could understand and respect—a kindness spoken quietly through discipline and strength.

My moment of panic began to pass as I realized I was surrounded by this special quality of the otherwise fierce Marines. I felt grateful to be a tiny part of it. For now, I accepted, I was home.

● **DAY 3**   Life in the women's tent promises to be interesting. There are so few female officers at the camp that they and some enlisted women all share a single space. There are twelve creaky and treacherously lopsided two-level bunks, enough for twenty-four women. Two were vacant prior to our arrival. My female teammate and I are making a cramped space smaller, both with our presence and our gear, and it is understandably not appreciated.

In the last few days' time, however, I have realized how many more issues are at play. We are contractors, paid an obscenely greater amount than our military for deploying to face similar dangers. We also provide capabilities to military forces that they do not possess on their own so we are, grudgingly, indispensable.

I wish I could tell the ladies that just before I left, I signed the paperwork to accept my own officer's commission immediately upon my return to the U.S. I would swear the same oath they had, with the willingness to return to war on the same terms they had. However, we didn't seem to be on chatting terms since our initial conversation.

When our new tentmates asked what we were doing at the camp, we happily explained the HTT mission. We thought of it as somewhat dry and academic, but it was met with not a small bit of envy. Most of the other women were logistics, aviation, or medical officers. They were incredibly educated and able, and they played vitally important roles in the Marines' mission, but none of them were ever allowed outside the confines of the camp.

"So you are saying that you cross the wire? That it's in your *job description* to cross the wire?"

Some ladies were wistful about the topic. "I wish I could go for a ride just once to see what's out there, beyond the camp, so I could tell my children that I did it. I could tell them about the people we came to help, or maybe about the colors of the bazaars, even if I just saw them from a window. That's my personal wish for this deployment. Otherwise, the camp is just a prison."

Other ladies were angry. "If you can go, can you explain what, exactly, prevents us? In order to be perceived well as Marines, we do everything in high heels and backwards. We need to excel beyond our brothers in fitness, in combat arts, in everything. We're officers, and we didn't join the Marines to idly stand by in the fight."

I wasn't sure how to respond, but I knew I had mixed feelings regarding women in combat. I was going out because I was among the few researchers both willing and qualified to conduct the HTT mission. Because the "pool" of such people was so small, some of us were bound to be female. I wasn't actually trying to take a stand regarding women in combat, nor was I anxious to have to face combat myself, should it find me.

It is now 3 AM and I am writing from a chow tent in some unknown part of the camp. As I feared, I never was able to find my way back to the unfriendly women's tent at night. It's just as well.

Even if I had miraculously located the tent, my big flashlight wouldn't be allowed after lights-out, and I wondered how I would find my bunk in the pitch blackness. I was also fairly certain that I wouldn't be able to manage the Hail-Mary running vault required to reach the top mattress if I tried it blindly. (Ladders appear to be an unnecessary luxury for Marines, and the top bunk is so high that you hit your head against the tent roof if you try to sit up in bed.)

I am on my third bowl of the tomato soup left out overnight for insomniac eaters. It lets me keep my place at a quiet table. I have found the perfect location to collect my thoughts and wait out my jet lag. I admire how the near-orange color of the soup compliments that of the Tang, also left out for late-night refreshment. The combination is growing on me.

● **DAY 4** The biggest problem of the camp has been brought to light thanks to the central areas between tents where smoking is allowed. Neighboring tents have begun to install creatively constructed benches around the smoking areas. This was quickly and vehemently prohibited by the camp's commander, based on the fact that

Marines sitting on benches gave the appearance of having nothing to do.

The sad fact is, for the most part, nobody does have anything to do. We have been utterly shocked to find no work for ourselves as we settle in to our new existence. It isn't that HTT work isn't needed, it is that Leatherneck is still so much in the process of building itself that no patrols are currently going out. Our sole purpose is to "go out," so we find ourselves stymied. Each of us is secretly anxious to test ourselves—to go out and return without fear.

Today we tried a temporary solution to part of our problem. If we can't go out, we might still be able to inform the commander of the Human Terrain situation of his area by interviewing those who came in. Local truck drivers are arriving daily, delivering supplies for the building of the camp.

While the Marines kept the incoming truck drivers "penned" in a secure area while their vehicles were inspected, we attempted to insert ourselves diplomatically into a somewhat tense situation. While most drivers were neutral or friendly toward U.S. forces, they still can't be treated as "safe" by the Marines because of the possibility of a bomber posing among them. However, the constant segregation builds resentment. We somehow had to appear neither distrustful nor vulnerable while mingling with the drivers.

I personally thought the truck drivers were quite brave. By delivering supplies to a U.S. camp, they were openly defying the wishes of the Taliban. Doing so invited retaliation. Still, one could never be sure if just one of them wasn't actually an enemy waiting to execute an attack.

We approached a group of several men, lounging and smoking. Their reaction to us as a team was interesting. They immediately reached out to shake hands and share quick smiles with our two men.

Lanky was in an Army uniform, and Pop was in the Indiana-Jones-type clothing typical of government employees attached to the military. Clearly, the Afghan gentlemen displayed no issues of discomfort with either a representative of the U.S. military or an American civilian. They were relaxed, jovial, and friendly.

Tex was dressed fairly conservatively, but she wore her short-sleeved T-shirt and let her long hair show. I, still waiting to assess of the liberalness of the area, was dressed with more modesty—my arms were covered in the available Indiana-Jones gear, and my hair was concealed. The Afghan men's reaction to both of us was the same. It was a combination of discomfort, disdain, and even a certain degree of revulsion.

They seemed obliged by the men who introduced us to shake our hands, but they did so with obvious reluctance. They literally recoiled from the touch. Then, as if sharing some joke, they laughed together as they wiped their hands immediately on one another's clothing, as if to "clean off the cooties." I found this fascinating. It was just this sort of detail I was there to learn from and record for analysis so that we could interact better on our next try.

I also found their reaction somewhat surprising, as I had expected that they would enjoy the opportunity to encounter foreign women, who were both culturally permissible and accessible for them to interact with and touch. I had assumed that men who rarely saw women to whom they were not related would be interested to see new faces. I had also wrongly assumed that they would be anything but put off at the rare opportunity to touch such a woman.

These assumptions were, of course, based out of my own cultural norms. I realized my perspective needed to be re-examined in short order. My goal, eventually, would be to try to see Pashtun culture through its own norms.

Despite their icy attitude toward me, I began to interview the men about where they had come from. They had made a perilous journey, and their truck had been hit by an insurgent rocket. They showed us the point of impact.

Then, I saw the most interesting member of the party peering uncertainly around a corner. A boy, about 11 or 12, had traveled with the men. I invited him out, and while he was at first distant and sullen, his eyes lit when he told us of his bravery in the face of the rocket-wielders.

I asked him why he had come, and he said he was accompanying his older brother. However, it turned out that none of the men in the party were, in fact, his brother. All were easily old enough to be his father. I considered if he was, perhaps, an orphan or a tolerated stowaway. I wondered who might be concerned about his having gone missing, and I hoped for his safety.

I wanted to keep an eye on him and try to better understand his story, but I must not have tried hard enough, as the boy slipped away amid the trucks and the noisy confusion. I had a strangely intense pang of regret.

Worrying that he might have been in some trouble or in need of help, I mentioned him to the guards.

I passed on how odd I thought it was that his story about traveling with family didn't fit. "Don't worry about him," I was told, "These guys sometimes travel with kids, and they seem fine. They'll get to where they belong. It's normal." Pop, who had spent prior deployments in Afghanistan, said as much, so I resigned myself to this unusual fact.

However, the day has passed, and I am still bothered. The boy seems to have been "okay" within the cultural norms I am just learning, but I still have the uncomfortable gut sense that I somehow failed that brave child. I suspect that it is just my unease at the idea of seeing any child in a war that has me disturbed. I am certain that I will soon meet many more.

● DAY 7   Unexpectedly, I connected with the ladies still unpacking in the tent over a topic about which all girls giggle and embrace, regardless of their differences. I was recently engaged! My teammate mentioned the fact, and suddenly there were congratulations and questions all around. I quickly found myself telling everyone about my favorite topic.

My fiancée, an HTT program member and a strapping example of a former Marine, was also in Afghanistan. When I said a difficult goodbye to him at the airfield in Kandahar, we both expressed that we hated to be unmarried much longer—especially as we were pulled our separate ways on different teams. We planned to start a family as soon as our deployments ended. (This produced delighted squeals from the ladies in the tent.)

My Marine and I had attended an impromptu party around a bonfire on the outskirts of the airfield, and surrounded by friends old and new, it seemed we were seeing exactly what our wedding should be. We could easily get a Chaplain to marry us, and maybe even a local Mullah as well. We would help the local economy by purchasing bread and roasting a goat to share with everyone, and we could dance the night away around the fire.

It was the most romantic notion that had ever played through my mind —a celebration of life and love amid the reality of war. It also appealed strongly to my more sensible side. Aside from the goat, I never could see spending big money on a wedding that you could later put toward a good washing machine.

The ladies pressed for the details of my dress, and I told them how my Mom, so wonderfully understanding and supportive, was finding it, sewing my veil, and shipping it, with all the decorations for the wedding, to Afghanistan. Though Mom couldn't be there, she would be in every detail. The whole tent got teary with me.

DAY 9 Things are becoming easier, and I am settling in. My team has won and defended our very own corner of "desk" space (really half a plastic folding table) in a command tent, which I can use for writing our research plans and reports. I spent most of the first week doing this in the two-foot high space of my bunk, or at my special Tang-and-tomato hideout. The cooks now wave at me there, and sometimes save me much-coveted croutons for my soup.

I am now seeing past the formality to the can-do cheerfulness of a few thousand Marines, and their motivation is infectious. Beginning to recognize me, enlisted Marines have started to "snap to" and beam smiles my way. "Good morning, Ma'am! Glad to see you!" Officers have begun to welcome me with unexpectedly cordial gallantry to the humble offerings of the chow tents.

I've found the boarded half-shelter where I can attend church. Strangers are quickly becoming friends as they strike up conversations and tell me stories of their lives back home. I am starting to feel truly welcome. Even in this Martian landscape, I realize I am in a place I could grow to love, not because of anything "lovely" here, but because of the people sharing the space.

Just like I have begun to know and like the Marines here, I hope that soon I will get to know and even build friendships with the local village communities. If even in this forsaken bit of land the kindness of humanity can flourish, I can't wait to see it in people beyond my own culture. I know I have bitten into the most starry-eyed conception of our mission here, but I see a truth to it.

My journey in Afghanistan will take me much farther out, to the Forward Operating Bases, and the even more remote Combat Outposts. However, now that its foreignness has worn away, Leatherneck itself has begun to impress me. I still tend to lose my way, but this has allowed me to discover that if you look up from the far reaches of the camp after dark, you find yourself drifting on an unsullied and endless blanket of desert beneath a perfectly black sky. It makes the stars seem completely unreal in their brightness.

Even though it's a sea of sand, it somehow still calls to the sailor's spirit in my Sicilian soul and soothes me. My great grandfather, who Mom taught me to call Nanu, was a proud and powerful sailor who brought our family to America, and he was fiercely patriotic regarding his new home. When I was little, Uncle Joe taught me the constellations by which Nanu could navigate and promised that Nanu would always be in the stars to guide me. The stars feel so close here I can't help but hope that Nanu is guiding me now, and that somehow I might make him proud.

My thoughts turn naturally to my grandfather, who in World War II had served in the Army as a standby typist in Burma, working with British forces. That's what he always told us, but it had only just occurred to me to wonder—what on earth was a standby typist? Was the typing in Burma so overwhelming that the regular typists just couldn't manage? Did a Jack Nicholson character occasionally burst into the room bellowing "You can't handle the typing!" and then my grandfather would take over?

After the war, my grandfather was a troubled, introspective, and incredibly funny man. He told stories of wildly implausible adventures he had had with his best friend, who called him only "Sahib." It simply means "sir" in a number of languages, including Dari, a language spoken in the country I find myself.

As I thought about it, it occurred to me that if even some small part of those stories were true, they were adventures no "standby typist" would ever have ever seen. It finally dawned on me what my grandfather had done for his country during the war. I sent him my thoughts of gratitude, and I hoped he would help lead my boots after his.

● **DAY 10** Shipments to the camp have lulled, and we have exhausted the pool of truck-driver interviewees. Our team leader has determined that we should scatter and link up with teams in-country that are already functioning in order to gain experience and to engage ourselves in useful Human Terrain work until Leatherneck becomes more operational.

It seems like a good idea. I am restless to get to work. I know I will have to patrol, and I am anxious to be rid of the nervousness of my first time out. Putting it off just makes the anxiety worse. I hope to return to Leatherneck and to my team experienced and even a bit "salty" in operating outside the wire.

Lanky plans to remain at Leatherneck, Tex will go north, and I will go south. Our miniscule team is already reduced today by one member, Pop, due to program issues back home. Those of us who signed on as contractors could either choose to be converted to sworn government employees or leave the program. The young father decided that while the risk of HTT work was worth the contractor salary, the potential cost to his family was not worth government pay.

His choice prompted each of us to reconsider the same personal decision. If I stayed, I would no longer be a high-paid contractor but the same kind of civil servant—or "Govie"—I had been years back when I began my career, though with the lucky caveat that my pay grade should take my education into account. Because of the timing of the conversion paperwork, however, I will lose the danger pay and extra pay for time-in-country that is a Govie's greatest bonus. Still, other HTT members who do not hold the position of Social Scientist are far less fortunate.

I needed and had truly counted on making and saving the contractor money. It would have been a life-changing solution to difficult circumstances. Now, having to choose to stay or go is forcing me to think through my own feelings a little more carefully. If the money is off the table and I still decide to stay, what are my actual motivations for being here?

Important as it was, I am realizing my desire to join the program was never primarily about the money. I was intrigued by the chance to combat the violence of terrorism—the extreme cruelty made possible only by the complete dismissal of the humanity of others—with a "weapon" as human as improving cultural understanding. The paradox spoke to me, and I was drawn in.

Now at this point, with my boots firmly on Afghan soil, I am committed to the mission, and I want to accomplish what I signed on to do. Plus, as I am coming to understand about myself, I do have a slightly reckless spirit. Once I have committed to something, I am not good at backing

Proud Papa.

down, even if it becomes in my better interest to do so.

Also, it seems as if my future leads from here. I am engaged and look-ing forward to my wedding in Kandahar. My Mighty Marine fiancée is in Afghanistan, and I will stay as long as he does.

For all these reasons, when a smiling officer stood by the flag and asked me to take the oath I knew so well, I could not find it in my heart to refuse. I hoped that Nanu and Grandpa would be proud.

● **DAY 11**   *"Salaam!"* I waved and nodded politely, leaning from the door of a tiny speeding helicopter. The surprised farmer smiled as we zipped by, only feet above his head. An enormously muscled gunner manned an impressive weapon at the opposite door, and he took to shouting a cheerful *"Salaam!"* to the people we passed as well. *"Salaam!"* we waved to small villages, and to the occasional wanderer in the desert.

The greeting, which means only "peace," was most sincere. "Peace, little village, peace," we mumbled quietly through our headphones as each town was swept from our view. It was a wistful prayer.

We were flying to avoid rocket and small-arms fire, so we followed the rolling terrain of the sand close to the ground. No one could see us coming over the rises to take aim until we were right upon them, and then we were suddenly gone again. In such a small and open helicopter, the experience was more like riding a speeding motorcycle just ten feet off the ground than like the sedate flight of a plane. It was exhilarating.

I was headed to a Forward Operating Base in Kandahar province called Ramrod to rendezvous with the team to which I was temporarily assigned. The coincidence was to my supreme delight, as my fiancée was newly attached to the Kandahar team. He was the man in whose arms I felt unquestioningly safe and protected, and I was flying toward them.

The assignment had a bittersweet complexity, however, as this was the team on which Paula had served. I was shocked to learn that they continue to operate in the same vicinity where she had met the sadistic attack. The shadow of the tragedy hung heavily over any effort by a woman to re-engage with the area.

At first, I attempted to think of Paula's story as an issue unrelated to gender. After all, any HTT member faced the danger of attack when operating in the villages. However, those with more experience in the area seemed to act on the notion that Paula's gender was a definite factor, almost as if her death through treachery and violence was reserved for those deserving of the most extreme contempt in the minds of Afghan extremists—women.

After Paula was evacuated, the program had chosen to reassign a male social scientist to the deeply shaken Kandahar team. No woman, HTT member or not, had been allowed to venture outside the wire in the area since. I was somewhat slow to arrive at the realization that I would be the first woman to take Paula's place.

Suddenly, I am in over my head and afraid. Everyone wants to end the nervousness of their first time outside the wire, but I had assumed that mine might be on a more reasonable mission—somewhere safe enough where my first outcome would most likely be a good one. I now regret "chomping at the bit" to go out.

CHAPTER **2**

Mamma Told Me
Not to Come!

● **DAY 12**

Tomorrow, the team will leave FOB Ramrod for the
even more remote Combat Outpost near where Paula
was burned. It is from that outpost that I am to embark on my first patrol.
I stayed up all last night, kept awake as much by the idea of so immediately facing the nightmare that had haunted me as by the roar and crash
of incoming and outgoing rocket fire. (To my surprise, rockets really do
have a red glare, and bombs do often burst in air.)

It was all good reason to reconsider my options. I thought again about
Pop, who had already left the program. I could do the same. I was a civilian and, unlike the military members around me, I had the option to leave,
stay safe, and forget the outrageous situation in which I had been placed.
In a few short days, I could be home, eating recognizable food, sleeping
in my own bed, taking hot showers, and hugging the adored giant of a
fluffy dog I missed terribly. It was hard to see a downside to this plan.

My Mom, who I loved so much and truly regretted causing such
worry with my crazy trips off to war, would be incredibly happy with me.
My fiancée would come home soon enough, and we would marry then,
even without the Mullah and the bonfire. Meanwhile, I would bake cook-
ies and send them to him like girls with any sense did. I didn't have to go
where Paula went, or charge into the danger of which I was so afraid.

A single persistent thought, however, began to erode an unfortunate
chink in my resolution to leave. *If no American woman returned to the area,*

33

then that one terrorist had accomplished something. The U.S. hesitancy to send a woman back unintentionally broadcasted a message that violent extremists still ultimately controlled what did and didn't happen in the area— not coalition forces, and more importantly, not the peaceful Afghans themselves whose lives had been dominated by the incredible violence of Taliban rule.

This was the same rule that had made the September 11th attacks possible. The same rule that caused women to be brutally tortured for the shameful crimes of men. My heart raged against terror wherever it took place, and here was one of its roots. It affected the innocent people of Afghanistan as it had impacted the good people of my own beloved country, and our two fates were inextricably linked.

If no woman returned, we were proclaiming that the Taliban still had latent power, and that the protection offered by U.S. presence could not be trusted. It encouraged the villagers' continuing secret loyalty to extremists, lest they be punished with the unbridled violence they knew so well. If the people stayed secretly loyal, then the Taliban was not defeated, just well-camouflaged, so that their insidious influence would go on indefinitely.

If I did patrol with the Kandahar team, my simple presence would be a show of defiance in the face of an extremist hold-out. It would wordlessly announce that no act of violence, no matter how horrifying or dramatic, would cause us to change our ways or to back down in our commitment. They could give us their best shot, and tragic though it was, it would change nothing.

I have a problem. Once I see a challenge, let alone an important one, I somehow become completely incapable of backing away. *Testa dura*— Mom always called me affectionately. Blockhead. She was right.

How committed was I to this fight? I came because something about terror enraged me above all else, and I wanted to feel as though I was contributing to the protection of innocent people. Was I willing only to offer academic observations from behind wire-rimmed glasses, or did I have large enough ovaries to make a stand myself?

My Mom had always taught me not to go looking for a fight, but *never* to give up once one found you. I certainly hadn't looked for this one, but once I "got my Sicilian up," my personal sense of right left me no option. I was going.

Typical moment.

● **DAY 13**   It was hard to escape, even momentarily, the shadow cast by past events. Soldiers from the Forward Operating Base had been disciplined for referring to Paula as "Barbeque." Now, when I passed, I heard the same reference sniggered, though couched in a way less likely to be reprimanded.

When I went for lunch, for instance, the biggest joke was, "Hey, there's fresh Barbeque in the chow hall!" The morbid humor always resulted in hysterical laughter, probably based more on the frayed nerves of the young men rather than any intended cruelty.

With my nerves similarly frazzled, I felt like laughing too when I discovered that my decision to go came with one more unanticipated risk. The logistical problems back at Camp Leatherneck were haunting me in unexpected ways. The camp was still so unfinished that it lacked a certified firing range. Theoretically, no one could carry a firearm in theatre without recently completing an official qualification on a certified range—no matter how extensive their background, level of experience with weapons, or qualifications might be elsewhere.

I had pestered the HTT program to set up an opportunity for deploying personnel to qualify before going overseas as most other programs did, but I was told over and over that I would have no problem finding a firing range as soon as I arrived in theatre. While that may have been true for those arriving at established bases, Leatherneck was another story.

I had assumed that I would qualify in Kandahar, but the team had stayed only in the rural areas without the necessary facilities. Now finding myself operating from a base with austere conditions that made the facilities at Leatherneck seem the height of civilization, I had another extremely difficult choice to make. I could either patrol without a firearm or abstain from participating in the work outside the wire that I had realized the pressing need to accomplish.

I stuck with my decision to patrol. Besides my commitment to the mission, two factors played into this. My life has been a series of the bizarre and I have rarely set out to do the things I end up doing. However, I have always had a sense that I was in the right place at the right time to do whatever it was I was meant to accomplish. I trusted there was a reason I was here now, being asked to do this in particular.

I suppose, in this small way, I understood a bit of the typical Muslim response to all questions and challenges. While generally it confounded me in others, it now comforted me in myself. *Inshallah*. Its meaning was somewhere between Doris Day's *"Que sera, sera"* and the prayer familiar in both Christianity and Islam, "Thy will be done."

Secondly, I perhaps could have been smarter, but I was in love, and in my case, the two rarely coincide. My Marine had appointed himself my bodyguard, and I felt I had every reason to trust him. Once, when we were being transported to an exercise in the Nevada desert, the open bus we were riding accelerated abruptly while I was still boarding, sending me flying away. My fiancée somehow reached out a massive paw, caught me in midair, and hauled me in over the rail before any harm could come to me.

The bus let out a round of stunned applause at the feat, and he secured my trust and adoration with that one swipe of his hand. Now, to say that I would not patrol unarmed when he swore to be nearby was tantamount to saying that I did not trust him anymore to protect me. He hinted that to do so would have hurt him unimaginably and damage the relationship I so treasured, so I relented.

Still, in life outside HTT, I frequently carry a gun, have always shot well, and have deep affection and appreciation for the safety a firearm provides. As I pulled on my uniform today and realized it was all there was—no holster to strap on next or sling to adjust—I suddenly experienced the ice-cold chill of extreme vulnerability. I was without even a pistol to tuck discretely at my side.

Fully dressed, I couldn't have felt more naked. However, I've been emphatically assured that at no point tomorrow will I be without my patrol and inner team surrounding me, so I should feel as comfortable as if I were armed with each and all of their weapons. (I have taken to repeating this over and over to myself.)

Afghan kids. (Photo courtesy Department of Defense)

CHAPTER 3

In the Clutches
of the Mullah

● DAY 14

I t was with the decisions of the past few days haunting my thoughts that I ventured into my first encounter with a rural Afghan community. Accompanied by a small group of young soldiers from the U.S. Army's 1st Infantry Division and additionally providing our own security to one another as a team, we set out from the small combat outpost ironically called "Hotel" in the Maywand district, and began moving in the formations that reminded me of a clumsily-choreographed Country Western line-dance intended to avoid land-mines—or to help avoid the entire patrol being taken out by a single mine if one of us should happen to misstep.

As the afternoon wore on and we trudged under our stiflingly heavy armor, we would wave to the groups of curious children that spied on us from hiding places. We knew they were reporting our positions and progress back to adults who may or may not wish us harm, but we smiled warmly to show that we meant them none. I carried candy and brightly colored pens, passing them out when I could. These small gifts, my notebook, and my grandma's pearl-handled stiletto with its well-worn blade, tucked close to my heart, were my only weapons.

We arrived at the village as twilight just began to cool the air, when most of the residents would be awaking from the afternoon rest they took in the heat of day. As protocol demanded, we stopped at the house of the most important local leader, the Mullah, to greet him and ask his permission to proceed in visiting with members of his community. His reaction upon seeing me seemed rather extreme. "A woman! A woman!" he shouted repeatedly with surprise and apparent delight.

While I found myself soon involved in a strange conversation with the Mullah, I noticed an odd phenomenon befall the men in my patrol. They were besieged by young men and boys. They were not violent but, bizarrely, almost fawning.

This was perhaps friendly, but dangerous nonetheless, because the youngsters surrounded the soldiers and team members, constantly touching their arms, their uniforms, their weapons, and not giving them the freedom or room to move or see around them. Because these fawners were "harmless," they could not easily be fought away. Endearing and childlike, they would insist on being shown a watch or a rifle over and over.

My fiancée walked away from me to show a curious young man how a rifle worked. The big Marine was flattered by the attention, and he suddenly felt fatherly toward the teenager. He and his rifle, however, had been my closest protection, and now both were yards away and otherwise occupied.

Meanwhile, ignoring all other topics of conversation, the Mullah spoke insistently to the translator, stating repeatedly that he must explain to me that "the Mullah likes women." When I responded pleasantly but didn't seem to grasp the full meaning, he insisted again, "the Mullah *likes* women."

"He likes sleeping with them," the embarrassed and exasperated translator finally blurted out. "He is not uneducated, and he actually, truly enjoys sleeping with women," he went on, as if this should be a revelation to me. I thought I understood the Mullah's meaning now, and that he was bragging to me of some exceptional sexual appetite or prowess.

The Mullah smiled, reassuring me enthusiastically. Somehow, it seemed that I was supposed to find it both surprising and a relief that he was openly attracted to women. I was again just beginning to encounter something entirely upside down from my own cultural norms.

The Mullah then took on a cast of sincere concern and the translator went on. "The rest of the men are uneducated here. It would be safest and best for you if you stayed and married the Mullah. You could remain in his house and be happy."

The translator, now almost unbearably uncomfortable with the subject, continued at the Mullah's insistence, saying, "His wives can attest that he sleeps with them. You must meet his wives."

At that moment, while utterly taken aback by this surreal conversation, I was physically overpowered. I had only barely nodded consent to the idea of meeting his wives, simply because it was a rare opportunity to encounter local women, which was a part of my job responsibility whenever it was possible. However, I was unprepared for what happened next. The Mullah swung me in strong arms through the door of his walled compound in one swift, unexpected motion.

In a single nightmarish second's passing, I found myself separated from my team and patrol. I was painfully aware of how easy a target I seemed—a diminutive woman, visibly unarmed. This swift isolation, we were taught, was how personnel are frequently taken when they are to be executed for propaganda purposes. It also seemed that the Mullah might be intent on "making me his wife" at that very moment. Either way, I had landed in a trap.

To my complete dismay, the patrol had made no move to stop the Mullah, nor did they follow. HTT had recently lost another member who unwittingly stepped into a space which, like the Mullah's imposing compound, had not been previously cleared of potential gunmen and explosives. The unknown possibilities beyond the door, everyone seemed to have decided, were too great a risk.

I could no longer hear the team outside the thick plaster walls. All I could hear were the wailing screams of the Mullah's wives and daughters, who appeared terrified over whatever violence they perceived was about to ensue.

As the Mullah stood blocking my escape, time seemed almost liquid, allowing me a few final thoughts of regret. If he was about to rape me, I would be compelled to fight desperately to one of our deaths. I then quickly realized it would have to be mine. If it was his, we could count the tenuous and important alliance of this village lost. Bloody retaliation against our outpost would be assured, and too many American lives would suffer for it. I couldn't fail to fight, but I couldn't afford to win.

If, instead, he had taken me to be the newest feature on a Taliban beheading video, I would be free to defend my life. However, without a gun, the probability of my success against the big Mullah in addition to whoever else might be there to assist with the video looked dim. I had a pang of regret for not wearing lipstick or earrings, so I could look my most presentable for the camera.

My mother and grandmother both had always told me never to go anywhere without lipstick and earrings. They warned me that you always got caught when you're not looking your best. Here I was, and they were right.

My problem lay in the fact that until this man's actions somehow identified him as an insurgent fighter or he made clear his intent to kill me, he could not be counted as an enemy—though it was always quite possible that any person we encountered might be one, as Paula's story had made too clear. I couldn't attack preemptively against him, the surprise of which may have been my only chance for survival. Instead, my actions needed to be founded on the assumption that he was an innocent man, simply acting as he saw appropriate, based upon his own cultural norms.

Though his actions were extremely threatening, to this point he had not *necessarily* done anything wrong. He was the prominent leader of a village that could be swayed either toward support of the Taliban or support of our forces. We could quickly make enemies of this village by any misstep on our part.

It was, oddly, just these cultural missteps that the Human Terrain Program had been created to identify and ultimately help avoid. Unfortunately, I had found myself directly involved in what was perhaps the most extreme confluence of cultural hot-spots imaginable—those of life, death, and sex.

A few more moments passed while I fully registered that no one from my patrol or team would be following me. Though my hand still hovered over my hidden blade, the Mullah remained still, so I turned my attention to calming the screaming women. With much bobbing and bowing and offerings of *Salaam*, I finally communicated that I intended no violence toward the ladies, and we all got past our shock at seeing one another. The Mullah, though he had not moved from his stance in blocking the way out, suddenly broke out in a smile and gestured as if to say "Perfect! Get to know each other!"

It occurred to me then that the Mullah might truly hope to keep me as a wife without the use of violence, and that he seemed to believe himself to be saving me from the "uneducated" men outside his walls—whatever that meant. A solution to the cultural stalemate began to form in my mind. I realized that getting out the door meant creating my own opportunity, though I needed to do so while I still had some chance of reuniting with my patrol.

So, using the few broken Pashto phrases I had learned to ask women about food and cooking, I settled in and started to ask what the ladies were making for dinner. I expressed interest, as best I could, in learning the Mullah's favorite recipes. Then, I allowed them to see what a dense and hopeless learner I was without a translator.

"*Tarjomaan! Tarjomaan!*" I kept repeating. "I just don't understand without a translator." Finally convinced of my intent to stay and learn, but exhausted with my linguistic ineptitude, the Mullah himself opened the heavy metal door he guarded and started to call out for the patrol to return with a translator. While the women remained silent watching my intended escape, I inched slowly and calmly for the opening.

When a male translator peeked through, the women began their screaming once again, and I feigned offense for my new near-sisters that a man would have looked into the Mullah's wives' quarters. To restore somewhat more culturally-appropriate decorum to the situation, I stepped out into the open street to speak with the translator. Then, clear of the door, I made a break to catch up with my team, who had proceeded a bit further along the route, and once again surround myself with well-armed soldiers. The deterrent finally worked, and to my utter relief, the disappointed Mullah did not follow.

This was far from the end of the patrol. Still without a gun, I actually had to use a simple hand-to-hand technique I learned from Krav Maga[1] to get out of the violent grip of another man of the village, angry about my being a woman walking freely, later that evening. He was close to breaking my wrist before he reacted with utter shock to the fact I was able to break his grip unexpectedly.

His shock itself is what allowed me to move away. As before, concern for Afghan cultural constraints put me in the position of having to free myself from the man while carefully refraining from going so far as to hurt him. This was a continually bizarre detriment in the context of a war.

For a man to be publicly bested by a woman would cause a degree of insult and outrage that would damage the vital "hearts and minds" effort we had sacrificed so much to win. Should I shame the man in the incident, the potential for damage and the endangerment of American lives would again be much greater than any risk might be to me. I was learning quickly how challenging it would be, as a female, to accomplish my purpose in this deployment.

Anyone on the patrol could have aided me without causing offense, as they were all men. Again, no one did. Instead, I was later heartily congratulated on my ability to take care of myself.

During what debriefing there was, the fact that I was able to diplomatically defend myself without the use of a gun was turned into evidence supporting the idea that it should not matter if I was allowed to qualify and carry a weapon in theatre. My observation that my lack of a gun contributed to the initial problem was dismissed. I couldn't help but laugh with resignation at the reversed logic.

Much later this evening, safely back in a tent, the male social scientist from the Kandahar team shook my still-sore hand for making it through the day and quietly asked me what I felt when I was pulled through the door of the Mullah's compound. He too had counted me for dead when he saw me disappear, just as I had thought, and he shared his concern about the same thing happening to him. I pride myself on remaining always truthful, but I lied tonight—both to him and perhaps to myself— when I said that I had consented to go in and calmly regarded the whole experience as an interesting research opportunity.

I couldn't help but wonder why he, if he shared my perception of the situation, had done nothing, along with everyone else. The incidents of my being isolated and unaided went completely unaddressed. However, on a quiet level—a level that it is unwise to explore now—I am afraid I am deeply unnerved by this fact.

I am in a situation where I can't afford to be distracted by my own hurt or fear. These feelings should be shelved away for later. My complete attention now has to be focused on present dangers if I want to survive, and present clues if I want to do my job well.

In a similar way, I am shelving away today's experiences for later analysis. The entirety of my first open encounter with southern Afghan culture has been bizarrely charged with the issues of sex and violence. However, I don't yet have the context to interpret any of it. For the time being, I have recorded it in my field notes, considered it a very strange day, and assured my exhausted self that future events will be different.

DAY 15 I sat in the chow tent the next morning, and after fully appreciating the fact that I was still alive, I thought a lukewarm bowl of Frosted Flakes had never quite tasted so good. I was savoring a spoonful when a young soldier approached politely. "May I sit with you, Ma'am?"

He was the picture of a little brother. Blonde haired, sparkly-eyed, and sincere, he looked far too young to be there. It seemed that his baby face had not yet seen its first shave, but here he was, an infantryman in a cruel and complex war.

I smiled and scooted to share a seat on the splintering wooden bench. His unit had seen too many casualties, and he almost certainly had lost comrades. "Would it be alright if I went ahead and asked you something?" he managed with shyness.

"Of course, buddy. What's up?"

"So, did you have to fight yesterday?"

"I did, but I didn't get hurt, and I managed not to offend anybody either."

"See, Ma'am, that's just what I don't get. Those guys attacked you, right? Why would you be so worried about their feelings? Do you want us to hold their hands and all sing Kumbaya while they try to blow us up? What are you doing here? What the hell are we all doing? I signed up to *fight* terror." The hurt of disillusion now shone in his eyes.

I struggled to find the answer for him. "It's all so difficult, Soldier, but there really is a reason for everything we're doing. There are a lot of different kinds of wars, and this one has particularly complicated rules, since our effort right now is a counterinsurgency."

"I've heard that fifty times already, but what is it supposed to mean to soldiers actually here? Why take stupid risks when we have the superiority in arms to kill them all? They don't hesitate to kill us. They didn't hesitate to kill my brothers out here."

His bravado dissolved and the boy in him sobbed. At the same time, I suddenly saw him as more of a man. I put a hand on his shoulder. "I'm sorry, my friend. I am so truly sorry."

He stiffened. "No, I'm serious!" he snapped against my coddling. "I want you to answer me."

For a moment, I was at a loss. I looked around the chow tent at the rows of perfectly matching soldiers. There was a place to begin. "I'll tell you how I learned to understand it, for what it's worth," I sighed and forged ahead.

"See, except for special reasons, when we fight, we make extremely clear who it is we are. We wear uniforms for instance, and our hair's all the same. That helps to protect innocent people. It says to the other side, 'Hey, I'm your enemy. So, if you want to shoot at somebody, shoot at me.'"

"That doesn't seem too smart," he said, suddenly looking at his own fatigues uncomfortably.

"It's not smart, but it is sort of, well, honorable, if you will."

"Like saying, 'pick on someone your own size.'"

"Very much like that, as opposed to what they do. They, like the cowards they are, conceal themselves in the midst of innocent people. They do everything to blend right in and hide in the villages."

"But they don't have money for uniforms," he said, thoughtfully. "I guess they could do something more identifiable though."

"It's not that, it's that they *try* to hide with civilians. They make it their goal. In that way, they basically use the good people in the villages as shields for themselves."

"It's sick when you put it that way."

"Sick is right. These extremists really don't care at all who they hurt in the furtherance of their cause—their own people included."

"So they hide with women, and babies, and kids and teachers and frick'n bread bakers and farmers who mean no harm . . . and hope we kill some of them instead?"

"That's the idea. Or, that we won't fight at all because we don't want to kill those good people. That's why we need a different way to fight. That's why a counterinsurgency works with the different rules you were asking about."

"And you're still not explaining how we are actually supposed to fight with our hands tied like that."

"Okay, so, even though most the people we meet won't be bad guys, they also won't be sure who to trust."

"Right . . ."

"So we need to convince them that we're the good guys—that we'll keep them safe and help them take back the power that the Taliban took away. If we don't convince them, they're going to side with the Taliban, because it will seem safer to them. It will make them our enemies when they could have been our friends."

"Great," he snorted, "We're all about making friends now? I came here to fight and win."

"We are fighting to win. I'm certainly here to fight and win. The thing is, a counterinsurgency is not won or lost by shooting, though as you know too well, plenty of shooting is sure to occur. A war like this is for the thoughts, feelings, and attitudes of the people—their hearts and minds, as it is often put rather poetically."

"See, now you're singing Kumbaya."

"Soldier, you're a bright guy, what do you want to do with your life once we're out of here?"

"I want to be a cop, maybe even join the FBI someday."

"I think you'll do just that. So, figure you are a cop and think of this a sort of like fighting gang members in an inner city. You wouldn't want to shoot up the neighborhood, because there are lots of innocent people."

"Of course not!" he exclaimed, suddenly a little horrified at his earlier comment about having the firepower to "kill them all." "That's totally the opposite of a Soldier's job!," he continued hotly, slapping the table and getting a splinter.

"See, you can't help it," I smiled, seeing the quality of the brave teenager before me. "You're honorable. You might call that knightly even."

He blushed, looking at his knees, but smiling at the compliment.

"Knightly," he repeated to himself softly, liking the word.

"Now think of the people in the neighborhoods. They know what's going on. They live there and they know who's who. They are threatened by the gangs, but they're a little of scared of the police too. They don't know who to trust, and they certainly aren't inclined to make enemies of the gang members. The gang members have them completely terrorized."

"Right, just like the insurgents here."

"Exactly. Now imagine what it would be like if the people in the neighborhood liked you—if they knew you and trusted you and understood that you would win and protect them against the threatening gang members who made their lives miserable and their neighborhoods violent."

"Yeah, they'd tip me off, because they'd want the gangs out of there."

"Right, and then what would happen?"

"Well, then we could find the gangs, take them down, and people would be safe to do whatever they wanted—to get on with their lives."

"Right, and if the gangs are stopped, then they can do less damage not just in the neighborhood, but all over—like drug trafficking across borders, for instance."

"Or like terror attacks, in this case here."

"And that's the definition of winning. It's putting an end to terror, just like you signed up to do."

"Huh. I like that a lot."

"Me too. Except in our case, you need to consider one more issue. Imagine you are doing all of this on Mars."

"Ma'am?"

"Instead of it being a neighborhood you basically understand, imagine you are in another world, where the things you say and do and think don't mean the same things to the people that they do to you. You need somebody to go learn what things mean to the other culture, and how to best make the friends you need in the neighborhood."

"So that's why you're here to do the touchy-feely culture stuff?"

"Yep. And it's also why I try so hard not to upset the locals."

"Okay, another question, then."

"Shoot."

"The guys you had to fight—I bet they all wanted to rape you, right?"

"I think one did, yes."

"One? So, you're out there, completely in the open, and out of all those men and teenagers who almost never get to see a woman, you mean each and every one of them didn't want to—you know . . . ?"

"Um, no." I chalked his observation up to the lively hormones of his youth.

"Well, they'd be crazy," he offered, while giving my dusty self an appreciative glance.

"Yellow light, Soldier," I said in half-teasing reference to the sexual harassment training the military receives. It's a light-hearted way to hint that someone is approaching the line of propriety.

He smiled abashedly and took up his tray to leave. "Thanks," he said, "for the talk."

"Anytime."

He turned back. "By the way Ma'am, you're not 'Barbeque' anymore. Just 'Barbie.'"

I choked on the last of my cereal as I laughed.

Kuchi family.

CHAPTER **4**

Bow-Wow Kuchi Coup

● DAY 21

The day's outcome revolved around a dog. He was an enormous sand-colored dog with round tufted ears like a bear—a breed that seems completely unique to this area. I think he was a good dog, but my Marines weren't so sure.

I am "home" again. Things have speedily improved at Leatherneck, so my team has been reassembled. I know my way around now. I see that a new, large, real-wood chow hall is being built. Navy Seabees (the Construction Battalion, or "C.B.'s") mill around, creating gyms and showers and offices that seem to appear overnight. I have mastered the vault to my bunk. Life is good. I am starting to feel like an old hand.

Today I patrolled the nearby area with the Marines for the first time. I think this might have actually been a few of these young men's first time out, because they seemed a little jumpy. We almost lost the dog.

It's funny that my first time out was so recent, and already it seems a lifetime past. I've been on a few mundane and uneventful patrols since my first. I am reassuring friends that they will make it through their first experiences at this point. Life seems to move quickly in a war.

Today's assignment was a simple "presence" patrol with the friendly goal of introducing the Marines to nearby residents. A bit of prior research told me that some families in the area were resettled Kuchi people—part of Afghanistan's unique gypsy population.[2] Some were also Pashtun. I couldn't wait to meet the neighbors.

We left early in the morning trying to avoid carrying our heavy packs through the desert in the heat of the day. For the first fifteen minutes of our walk, we saw absolutely nothing but dunes. Then the dog bounded out at us seemingly from nowhere.

He skidded to a sandy stop squarely in front of us and barked with his booming voice. It wasn't so much an "I-intend-to-eat-you" bark as a "you're-strange-here-and-I'm-not-sure-about-you" bark. My Marines, unfortunately, saw it differently.

"You get the #$!*&%#*$%# out of here," they snarled and shouted at him. The dog, who had been unsure about us, now made up his mind that we were hostile. He snarled back. The Marines jumped.

It has always been my experience that the bigger, stronger, and more intimidating a man is, the more he is prone to be frightened by a dog. I have a huge dog, and big men are compelled to run from him or challenge him while little children throw their arms around his fluffy neck and hug him. Now my Marines were reacting to the dog as though he was a threat.

"Get him out of here or I'm shooting that thing!" they yelled louder. The dog barked louder and grew more menacing.

"That's not authorized. Don't waste the ammunition," the Sergeant commanded.

"I'm shooting it before it bites me!," a few Marines yelled back with sincerity. Rifles rose to the ready.

Something was terribly wrong, and it had more to do with people than the dog. Before deploying, I learned as much as I could about the Kuchi. To them, a dog was as valued as a family member, and killing one was an offense equal to killing a person. Because Kuchi people were nomadic, their dogs were relied upon to protect the camels and goods they sold, and to keep people safe as they were exposed to the dangers of the road.

The Kuchi depended enormously on their dogs, and to harm one would be to deprive a family of one of its most valued assets. It would make instant enemies of the people immediately surrounding our camp, which couldn't be good for us. This was the kind of thing HTT was here to prevent.

The Marines seemed unaware that our relationship with the local area currently rested on the furry shoulders of the dog. I had to stop this, the only way I knew how.

"Whooooo's the barky dog? Who's the biiiiiiig barky dog?" I mustered all the delight and affection into my voice that I would give to my own dog. The dog cocked his head in an unmistakable "huh?"

I walked up between the Marines and him. "Yes, you're a gooood barky dog. You're such a good guard doggie, aren't you? Yeeeees you are!"

"Ma'am," the Sergeant put in, trying to cope with the fact that I had apparently lost my mind. "He doesn't speak English."

"He doesn't speak Pashto, either," I continued in my sing-song tone. "He's just listening to me talk to him. Aren't you, you Kuchi poochie? You Pashtu puppy? Yes you are!" Eyes rolled, but the Marines got my idea.

"Now you go home and tell your people we're here," I tried. Everyone liked that direction. "Yes, good doggie, you go home," they chimed in. We clapped briskly and pointed cheerfully away in the direction he had come. The dog understood.

The dog ran ahead of us to a Pashtun dwelling, so it turned out he was not a Kuchi dog after all. Still, shooting a neighbor's animal is never a good way to say hello. When we arrived at the compound, we introduced ourselves and the dog bounded up to me.

"Oh, very sorry about that!" the owner of the household said. "Just throw a rock at him and he'll keep to the wall. Here, I'll do it."

The owner pelted the dog, and mimicking their father, his little boys started a game by doing the same. The dejected dog retreated, and I was compelled to ask why they would hurt him, since he seemed to be such a good guard for their home. The question made me seem daft to the Pashtun man.

"He's a *dog*," the owner replied, as if this explained the matter to me. "It's in the Koran," my Afghan translator finally added helpfully. Then I remembered.

A story in the Koran tells of how angels wouldn't enter a house if a dog was in it. Because of the passage, there is a common logic in Afghanistan that dogs must be somehow offensive if they keep away angels. I've always interpreted the passage to mean that a house doesn't need angels to protect it if it already has such a good guardian as a dog—the angels must trust the dog to do the job.

I thought it was sad how the Koran was interpreted in this case to allow for the worst treatment rather than the best—for cruelty rather than kindness. However, it is my job here to learn and to keep my feelings to myself. One of the most important skills one can have in HTT work is the constant attempt to mitigate his or her own natural value judgments, and I take this challenge seriously.

We spoke for a while at the compound. The man would not allow me to visit with his wives, but he was happy with us because the run-off sewage from our camp was creating a fertile pool near his house. Things were growing on their own. We tried to explain why that water wouldn't be the best to use, but that we could try to assist in the family's farming. The explanation didn't go over well, but we left on friendly terms.

Pashtun pup.

Still, as we walked on, I continued to be confused by the small matter of the Pashtun family's attitude toward animals. About a mile from the complex that the dog guarded, I saw a camel. It wasn't a Kuchi camel, with a pretty bright bridle, but an unkempt one, hobbled by having one leg tied bent at the knee, so he stood on only three feet. He hopped miserably.

I wondered why he was not penned but tied in such an uncomfortable way. I also wondered why he was kept so far from people. Had he actually walked so far on his three feet? Would his owner go out and bring him home? I jotted my confusion in my notes.

Later, I actually did meet a Kuchi family nearby. They told the story of how they were forced to settle in a Pashtu-style village because the Taliban had made it too dangerous for them to travel on the roads. The Taliban enforced their intolerant laws at roadblocks, and women who weren't appropriately veiled or even appropriately deferential—as Kuchi women rarely are—were beaten savagely. Men would be similarly punished for equally minor infractions.

The Kuchi were good Muslims, but they didn't subscribe to all the culturally-based Islamic practices of the Pashtun. Kuchi women were seen openly as the families traveled. Compared to Pashtun women, this made them shockingly and scandalously free. The thought brought a smile to my face.

The men of the household had no problem with me visiting their wives and daughters. I found myself chatting easily among the women—who treated me as an immediate member of their gossip clutch. I felt drab compared to them, who wore tatters in every clashing color of the rainbow, and managed to look glamorous doing so.

I liked these families. The fact that the Kuchi treated even their dogs with kindness spoke volumes. I hoped that taking back control of the country from the Taliban would have the happy side effect of returning these people to their traditional ways.

Young farmer—a hero of Afghanistan.

CHAPTER 5

"So, What's a Nice Girl Like You Doing in a Place Like This?"

● DAY 25

The early spring is quickly becoming summer, and the heat is now so unyielding that it is nearly impossible to sleep. If anyone should be so lucky or exhausted as to manage, they will soon be awakened by the crackling and squealing of loudspeakers that precede the prayer calls from faraway mosques. Sound carries long and clear across the desert. Unlike the beautiful and ornate calls I remember hearing when I served on the Arabian Peninsula, these are short, gruff, and surprisingly lacking in melody. They seem more a demand than an invitation.

In fact, if too few people come to prayer, one local *muezzin* occasionally wakes the congregation by firing a few shots into the air. I always worry about the bullets hitting someone—maybe even a child—on their deadly way down. A bit shockingly, that favorite Muslim attitude to almost everything, *"inshallah"*—let whatever is God's will be done—seems to resolve the issue for the villagers.

It is because of restless nights like these that I have gained the habit of wandering, eventually finding a quiet place to sit and watch the moon in its almost-touchable closeness. *Inshallah.* What a strange sense of humor God must have, I thought, for His will to have somehow led *me* here.

I am not the kind of girl who anyone would easily believe had any business in this war or any background to do the work to which I am assigned. In fact, I do, but how I arrived at these things is a story almost stranger than my participation here and—in its own way—contributes to it, as well.

The truth of the matter is, I'm an opera singer. At four years of age, I fell in love with the opera *Carmen*—yes, a slightly inappropriate fixation for a preschooler—and from that point on have wanted to spend my life singing the character. This obsession was predated only by my love of the Spanish guitar, which I began studying when I was three. Both art forms are expressions of my Sicilian and Spanish cultural heritage, which I have always embraced with immense pride.

In the miniscule world of classical music, I actually have a notable career, both as a guitarist and a singer. I have given a solo recital at the Kennedy center. I've performed for dignitaries like the Prince of Spain

First opera.

(several times—before he was married and while he was at his most devastatingly handsome). I've played major guitar concerti with a number of orchestras, and I have over a dozen CD's to my credit. I tour nationally and have sung leading roles in operas in Italy and the U.S. Between deployments, I even provided an operatic vocal track for a CD featuring Kanye West and John Legend.

A chance at an opera career can only be achieved with extensive training, so years ago I sought to find the voice teacher who could render me *Carmen*-worthy. Eventually, I had the fortune of being accepted by Janice Pantazelos, head of the Chicago Studio of Professional Singing. Janice's impact on my voice and on my life would be profound. However, a major problem existed in that the studio was located in Chicago. I am from Santa Fe, New Mexico. I was nineteen, and I needed a plan. I never thought it would involve two wars.

Publicity shot for my first career.

That year, while playing flamenco in one of the Santa Fe tapas bars where I worked my way through college, I was "discovered" by the head of a major record company. I won't name the label because of what happened next, but for a moment I was slotted for being the next "it" thing. At that time, I actually possessed the teenage prettiness that we all do so briefly, could sing low and sultry torch songs as only a bar room can prepare one to sing, and could play the guitar like a woman possessed.

I recorded a new CD for the label and was scheduled immediately on tour to play the *Concierto de Aranjuez* with a full symphony—a preliminary step in a major national marketing plan for the album. Shortly before the tour began, my Mom and I were in a severe car accident with a drunk driver. Mom's selfless instincts saved both our lives.

Though we were gratefully alive, I had two injuries. My face was sliced open and mangled on the left side, and I had a "closed head injury," meaning my brain function would be disrupted. I could not remember basic things, but I could remember how to play the *Concierto de Aranjuez*, so I went on tour. With a stack of triumphant reviews and newspaper photos that showed me playing dramatically in profile (so that my Frankenstein-fresh stitches were hidden), I returned to the record label to begin the national launch of the album. "Sorry, my dear," the executive said after staring at me in complete silence, "but you used to be the total package."

With my appearance "ruined," my record was dropped. I realized I needed a new plan. This time, I wanted to possess something that couldn't be taken away so easily. I began to think that a Ph.D. might ensure a more stable future, regardless of my looks or lack thereof. At nineteen, prior to the *Aranjuez* tour, I was just completing my Master's degree. I had completed my B.A. at eighteen after graduating from high school at fourteen (as a result of being expelled—which is another long story that belongs elsewhere).

However, because of the head injury, while I retained my reasoning and memory, I hardly knew how to dress myself, tell time, or add two and two. Rather than "accept a new normal," I worked to relearn the things my injury had taken from me. I found myself at the community college, taking remedial courses. Eventually, I returned to the level of functioning where I could pass the GRE with the scores required for application at every Catholic girl's dream school.

With the theme music from the movie *Rudy* echoing in my mind, I applied for doctoral studies at the University of Notre Dame. I had an idea for an interesting dissertation topic, and I hoped that someone there would be receptive. I had always suspected a link between the Flamenco guitar music I grew up performing and the ritual prayer music of the *Penitentes* of northern New Mexico. If I was accepted to Notre Dame to research this, I would be only a short train ride away from the voice teacher with whom I so desperately wanted to study in Chicago. Plus, I would have a room, food, and a stipend just big enough to allow me to afford my lessons if I used it for nothing else.

The plan worked, with one major surprise. It wasn't the Music department that wanted my research, or the Institute of Latino Studies, to which I had applied, but the Theology department that welcomed me.[3] I couldn't absorb this.

Notre Dame's doctoral programs in Theology are renowned, small, and incredibly competitive. Most doctoral students had majored in the subject their entire academic career, and I wasn't the kind of girl anyone could picture in the Theology department of anywhere. However, academically, I was serious as anyone could be.

I had excelled in my studies before the accident, but Notre Dame was going to stretch me in ways I could not have anticipated. In the end, I had to take my research in a new direction to fit the parameters of the program of which I became a part. Though many strange turns that had guided my path so far, this alteration in plans was perhaps the most critical in my eventually finding myself in Afghanistan.

A major part of my research began to center on the history and culture of the three religions that converged in medieval Spain—Islam, Judaism, and Christianity. I became interested in why the three cooperated when they did, and what motivated them to violence when they committed it. I found history reflected in the faith traditions of living descendants of those who fled the Spanish Inquisition to northern New Mexico. As I became interested in people, rather than documents, as sources, I began to become engaged with ethnographic field technique and other means of eliciting people's guarded stories.

All of this began before September 11th, but as I sat on the 7th floor of the Hesburgh Library, fighting tears of horror as I watched the second tower fall on a tiny TV with my classmates, I understood what was happening. From that moment, I began to think about my research in a new light.

Simultaneously, while I was at Notre Dame, I ran into a friendly Army officer who drove a fast red convertible. The kind of car he had didn't impress me nearly as much as the fact that he had a car. I did not. I often walked for groceries in the brutal South Bend winters. When I was with him, listening to him tell me about the Army Intelligence program and how I should join, I did not have to walk.

Nevertheless, I really was listening, and his words started working on

Mom and Angelo and me at Notre Dame.

the grateful and patriotic streak in my Italian-American soul. I had a horrendous fight with my Mom, who I adored. We had almost never fought before, and I was stunned by her vehemence on this one matter. She had never asked a promise from me, but now she demanded just one—that I never join the military. I know she was simply worried over my safety. Rather than hurt her, I made the promise.

In the meantime, I completed my dissertation at 24 and graduated from Notre Dame as the youngest person ever awarded a Ph.D. from the institution. I signed with an agent who booked concert and lecture tours for me on the university circuit. I was making a respectable living as a classical musician, which is a feat, given how impossibly small the industry is. But war was underway, and convertible-man's words continued to eat at me.

Then, the elusive possibility of mainstream musical popularity appeared

El Duo Duende *in our days of "Flamenco Steel."*

again. After over 20 years of never seeing one another, the only person who ever influenced my guitar playing called when he began to hear my name on the concert circuit. It was Craig Alden Dell, the teacher I had when I was three years old. He was a reclusive but brilliant player who was a favorite of both Segovia and Sabicas, the diametrically-opposed kings of the classical and flamenco styles. Within a week of getting reacquainted, we performed together and were greeted with an uproarious crowd reaction at the West Coast Guitar Festival.

We were an entertainingly odd pairing but an ideal duet, and we had representation almost immediately. Television and news features abounded. Reviewers were wildly complementary, referring to us as a modern Presti & Lagoya. (You *really* have to be a music geek to know the reference, but it is very flattering.)

Then, in a last-minute decision as headliners for the East Coast Guitar Festival, we performed our flamenco set on rock-style steel-stringed guitars. It was an obviously reckless idea that resulted immediately in bloody hands and damaged instruments, but the drama caught audiences on fire. Two "El Duo Duende" CD's were issued immediately, one titled "Flamenco Steel," for which there was even a promotional tie with Harley-Davidson! We were poised for a popular crossover, when a shoulder injury requiring immediate surgery and prolonged recovery meant Craig could not tour. CD's do not sell without concerts to promote them, so no income would come from the duo.

Simultaneously, my parents separated, though they remained fantastic friends, when my father, with great integrity, came out as gay. With a situation drastically changed and our finances precarious, Mom and I made an agreement to work together to hang on to the Santa Fe property that was home. However, with the end of the duo, my musician's salary seemed clearly too erratic to make my monthly commitment.

A surprising solution presented itself when an earnest man in a turban appeared in a television commercial. His words echoed those that the Army officer with the red convertible had spoken not so very long ago. The FBI, with their regular federal paychecks, was recruiting heavily for individuals with advanced degrees and cultural/religious expertise. I soon found myself in a tasteful grey suit—a far stretch for my usual sense of style, which typically involved leopard print—and going to work just outside of Washington, D.C.

I trained as an intelligence analyst at the FBI Academy and was assigned to the Iraq Unit, where I was soon directly involved in counterterrorism issues both overseas and on U.S. soil. We were the real-life model for the wildly-exaggerated television series *24*, which was popular at the time. ("Agent Jack Bauer" and producers from the show would actually get cleared to visit our work location. The show's "CTU" was the

Bureau's "CTD," of which the Iraq Unit was a vitally important part due to U.S. war efforts.)

Though I can't say a great deal more, I was very proud to contribute to the counterterrorism mission in particular. I was also exhausted, as I would work long days to free up certain Fridays to allow me to travel to perform concerts and return to work without missing time—but Mom and I were succeeding in our commitment to hang on to Santa Fe.

Then, as it turned out, I ended up going to Iraq to avoid jail. Bizarre as it seems, it was perhaps the only set of events that would have ever made peace between my Mom and I over the matter. It, and all that followed, was also the only set of events that could ever have lead me to Afghanistan—a possibility that had not yet even appeared on the horizon of my thoughts.

A request was circulating for FBI personnel to deploy to Iraq in support of the Joint Special Operations Command. Given that command's responsibilities, it was an incredible opportunity. I considered volunteering and was preliminarily selected for a rather coveted slot. I reasoned that I wasn't joining the military, just helping.

There were good reasons to go. I was intrigued by the prospect of seeing the culmination of my education and work play out "on the ground," and I didn't feel right shying away from risks that some of my colleagues were willing to take. Plus, the overtime and danger pay meant that I might be able to afford to return to Chicago to study with Janice more frequently when I came home—a dream that my grey-suit wearing life seemed to be taking farther and farther away.

My friends in the unit, trying to get in their best shape before deploying, took to organizing an extreme fitness plan. They invited me to join in while I continued to consider my decision. I was fit only because I did not have a car and couldn't afford much food. I walked 4.5 miles to work and 4.5 miles back every day, and I took up running for a faster commute.[4]

However, I understand now that someone my size and shape was never intended to do things that 6'-something ex-military muscle men do easily. I enjoyed watching them do it, but I broke my foot trying. Then, not realizing it was broken, I ran until I damaged it to the point that I was relegated to a ridiculous contraption of a cast by evening.

It was three days before Christmas when I broke my foot. The next day, I was scheduled to visit the dentist, who botched a procedure to the point that, between my foot and my teeth, I was dizzy with pain. I consoled myself with the assurance that on Christmas Eve, I was flying home.

I stood in the airport security line hurting and dazed. I almost never take medication, but I was on a cocktail of pills for my various issues. When I approached the screener, she asked if I had any metal on my person. With my mind completely blank, I said no.

I walked through the metal detector and beeped. The screener asked why. I guessed that my walking cast had metal parts. She waved me through and "wanded" me. I still beeped. My broken foot didn't beep, but my bra beeped. She gave me a shy pat-down, and found nothing. "Well, that's one heck of an underwire," the screener observed to me as she waved me out of the checkpoint.

As I walked into the terminal, I slowly processed how strange a conversation that had been. Why was the screener so interested in my bra? Then it occurred to me. The knife I had casually stashed earlier was still there. If only I had changed my clothes as I had intended, I would have remembered to take it out.

Of course, this was not Grandma's beautiful protection knife that I would wear in Afghanistan. This was a little pocket knife I carried as a family memento from our last picnic. It, like my rosary and some cash, was tucked in my bra because my outfit lacked pockets and I wasn't carrying a purse.

I spun on my heel (the good one) and returned to the screener. "Ma'am, ma'am!," I called out in earnest, suddenly horrified that I had violated a security rule, "I'm so sorry! I completely forgot, but I had this on me. Let me give it to you now."

"You need to wait here while I get my supervisor," she responded sternly while snatching the sentimental little knife Mom had given as we lunched on the lawn and laughingly struggled to open a bottle of wine when I graduated from Notre Dame. The supervisor came out and offered to get me a FedEx envelope so I could send the knife home.

The screener fumed and took him aside, making wild gestures. Shortly, I realized that the screener had called the Airport Police. They descended on me and kept referring to the "weapons incident" on their radios. I was being viewed as a potential terrorist by the Police. For the first time in my life, I was arrested and led away.

Eventually, a nice Policewoman feeling the Christmas spirit released me on my own recognizance if I agreed to appear in court after the holidays. In frantic tears, I made a phone call. "Mom, I just got arrested!" Mom, despite all her efforts to be sympathetic, started giggling.

The more I tried to explain how it had all happened, the harder she started laughing. The more earnestly I described how this was going to ruin my life, the more into hysterics she slipped. "Just come home, Chica," she managed to get out. "God will help, and it will work out fine."

I returned to DC after the holidays fortified by my family's encouragements, missing some teeth, and determined to hire a lawyer who would work for what little savings I had. I also looked up the violation with which I was charged. It stated that no person was allowed to carry a switchblade or a Bowie knife in the secure portion of an airport. I was innocent of the charge! My little picnic knife of perfectly legal dimensions and features.

Instead of offering any word like this in my defense, however, my lawyer put me on the stand and asked, "Have you ever been physically attacked?" He must have been trying a fancy lawyer tactic to make me seem innocent. (I didn't need to seem innocent. I actually was.)

When I seemed surprised by the question and hesitated uncomfortably, he asked with blunt impatience, "Have you ever been violently raped?" I was prepared to speak about blade lengths and product specifications. Taken aback, but finding myself under oath, I answered a reluctant but honest "yes."

Things could have not gone worse for me from that point. The prosecutor launched an unimaginable tirade into my character. Knowing absolutely nothing about me (because my lawyer had said nothing), he painted me as a revenge-obsessed woman who carried around a tiny legal picnic knife so I could attack an arbitrary innocent victim in an airport when I finally "snapped." Shocked at both the absurdity and the cruelty of his statements, I found unexpected tears streaming down my cheeks, which he used deftly to prove his point.

Gavel swinging, the judge swiftly declared me guilty and sentenced me to six months in jail. Again, no help came from my lawyer. However, following the verdict, it was finally permissible to mention my federal employment. I begged the lawyer to say anything that might serve in defense of my character. I suggested mentioning my degree in Theology, my exemplary previous record, or my loyal federal service. What my own lawyer said was this: "Even though this is clearly a woman of questionable moral character, she may be deploying to Iraq, and a six-month sentence would prevent her from fulfilling this service to the country."

I was not yet actually scheduled to deploy. I still had that decision to make, and it truly depended on making peace with my family. The judge gave me an option.

I could be booked as guilty but allowed to go Iraq. However, if I chose not to go or did not complete the full length of my deployment, I would be obligated to serve out the entire six-month sentence in jail. Just like in the old movies, I could either go to war or to jail.

I had no money left to appeal, and given the way the trial had gone, I couldn't be sure a new trial would go any better. My lawyer assured me it would not given my "background," which would inevitably come up again. He himself had bought completely into the prosecutor's argument and urged me to take the judge's deal. "Just go downstairs now and let yourself be booked."

Still, I had a few days to decide what I would do, and I needed to clear my head. My heart stung at the idea of being handcuffed, fingerprinted, and held to bargain my own release. I almost wanted to go to jail rather than call myself "guilty" in the particular way the prosecutor had.

I hobbled outside the courthouse emotionally drained and hungry. It was almost three o'clock in the afternoon, and I hadn't even eaten breakfast. Like a mirage, there was a hot dog vendor on the street ahead of me.

I love hot dogs inordinately. For five dollars, I could have two dogs, a bag of chips, and a soda. I had spent all my savings and my whole monthly budget on the lawyer, but I had five dollars. (Yes, it was tucked in my bra.) It was literally my last five dollars until I was paid two weeks later, but at that moment, I couldn't think of anything more worthwhile on which to spend it than that feast.

I got my hot dog special and headed for the train back to work. As I stood waiting for the train and trying to work out my decision, I took one glorious bite. Then, an angry woman in a security uniform approached me. "Miss, there is *no* food allowed in this Metro station," she said. I apologized profusely for having forgotten the rule and offered to leave.

"You won't be walk'n anywhere in this station, even to leave, while you're carry'n that food," she said. Then she pitched my lunch into the garbage. "Maybe *now* you'll remember for next time," she added with a flourish.

I said a silent prayer that one of the homeless denizens of DC would find those delicious dogs before they got cold. The security lady kept a close eye on me as I left, just to make sure I didn't make a break to reclaim my lunch, which I peered back at sadly.

I made a phone call. "Mom," I said despondently, "they took my hot dogs," as if that explained everything. This time she didn't laugh. Then I did explain everything. "Do you know what you're going to do?" she asked gently. Though I was truly sorry that deploying was against her wishes, I felt that I only had one real sensible option.

"Mom, forgive me. I'm going back to turn myself in, and then I'll have to go to Iraq." Instead of fighting with me, her words were the first reassuring ones I had heard all day. "Don't worry, Chica. God will help, and it will turn out fine. Besides, it's very *Carmen* of you, going to jail and all. Don't flirt with the guards. Or maybe do." This time I laughed.

I thought of Carmen, walked with my head high, signed some paperwork regarding fines and fees, and turned myself in for booking. As I was led away and fingerprinted, I smiled and shared wry winks with the new friends I was making in holding. I had the tasteful grey suit and they had the thigh-high faux-leather boots, but it seemed we now shared the label of "women of questionable moral character," and I suspected it was as unfairly earned by them as it had been by me.

Though it would be several months before I even began considering going to Afghanistan after Iraq, this was one of my first windows of insight to the far more unreasonable experience of women in Afghanistan —an experience that would later become critical to my understanding of the people I would eventually come to know. I wasn't guiltless. I had made a very real mistake by having the knife. However, it wasn't my possession of the knife that had convicted me as a criminal—it was the dispersion cast upon my character based upon a circumstance beyond my control and in some way essentially related to my gender. This dispersion would never have applied to a man.

I made it back to work by early evening, and my Unit, as usual, was still there. I told them the court's findings and officially signed my intent to deploy. (The podiatrist had already given medical clearance on my broken foot, saying it would be healed by the time we left.) I felt resolved. I then tried to subtly scour the facility for food that might have been left over from any office parties. I almost broke down in tears again when I realized with what kindness my boss had saved me a plate.

I quickly found myself in full-scale pre-deployment training, even earning a Tactical Operational Medic (level 1) certification. By spring, we were aboard a C-130, making a heart-stopping "corkscrew" landing to avoid rocket fire, into Iraq. Oddly, the only thought that filled my mind was "Wheeee!" I soon realized, with some surprise, that I was happily in an element I didn't even know was mine. I was assigned to a tiny group, made up of individuals from all different services, engaged in amazing work.

While I can't give their names, or explain the incredible work they did to protect innocent lives, I can say something about who they were as people, and the ethos of the community they represented. This insight was the second essential bit of understanding that would eventually see me to Afghanistan. Upon arriving, I assumed that welcome into the group needed to be earned, and as a complete newcomer to the situation, I did not expect it.

However, instead of "hazing" me or treating me like an outsider, they immediately treated me not only well, but like a favorite sister. They dissolved in tears of good-natured laughter over chow after I contritely explained that I was there to avoid jail. They took to calling me "CC"—a nickname that I had earned back at the academy.

The day after I arrived, incoming enemy fire landed uncomfortably close to the location of our little group. A mortar landing too close produces a sound you actually feel rather than hear. Your ears don't fully perceive it, but your stomach and muscles turn briefly to gelatin before your mind can discern what has happened. By the time it does, the impact is over and you're still alive. While it was not an infrequent occurrence, it is odd to experience for the first time. Such a close call could set one's nerves on edge, if it is not dealt with in exactly the way my wise new friends did for me.

"First time, Cardinalli?" the soldier next to me asked with a wide grin. I nodded coolly, trying my very best to look seasoned. "Nice Job, CC!" he hooted. Everyone took up barking and yelling and slapping my shoulders. "Oorah, CC! Hooah! Hooyah! That's the way to show 'em!" A group of people intimately familiar with far worse than what had just happened were heartily congratulating me for doing nothing. The situation became a momentary little celebration of my welcome into the group—one which we repeated whenever someone new came aboard.

I still didn't know, but each of these experiences would soon become indispensible to my ability to function in Afghanistan, and were leading me inevitably there. Iraq changed things, and changed who I was as a professional. The operational tempo itself was enough to change anyone. 16-hour work days, 7 days a week was a fairly typical schedule, and most of those hours were filled with a desperate, oh-please-God-let-this-work, kind of stress.

We were responsible to very high-level authorities, and it was a regular expectation to interface with them (so I had to worry about my hair looking right, in addition to everything else). Unfortunately, the work itself can't even be compared to a fictional movie or television show as the work in the Iraq Unit was. I returned home with the Joint Service Civilian Commendation Medal, which I treasure not for the honor but for the memory of the people I worked with and what we accomplished together.[5]

Iraq also changed something unexpectedly and led me in a new direction. Suddenly, I became someone whose expertise was actively courted by high-paying defense contractors—someone whose experience was respected, not only academically, but militarily as well. Even as I sat happily at work in Iraq, contractors would make unsolicited and aggressive offers of new jobs. However, I thought I was too high-minded a civil servant to accept contract work.

Nevertheless, as a few unfortunate developments began to evolve back home, I began to rethink my attitude, especially as I was presented a fascinating offer that seemed like it was somehow written specifically for me. The offer, however, required deploying again, and this time it would be to Afghanistan. The experimental U.S. Army Human Terrain Program was seeking Ph.D.'s with prior deployment experience who had a background in cultural or religious studies, were familiar with ethnographic field methodology, and, perhaps most importantly, felt some personal connection and desire to help both the U.S. military and the people of the countries where we found ourselves involved.

How truly bizarre. Thanks to having gone to Iraq, and to all the previous experience that led me there, I had become a person who fit that description precisely. Life had actually groomed me for the HTT position in Afghanistan far more than I then understood. From training in research skills for academia and analytical skills for war, to gaining an intimate perspective on the character and purpose of the military, to knowing first-hand the experience of criminality based in part on gender violence—a mild version of the attitudes toward females and sex that horribly persecuted Afghan women know too well—it was as if everything I had learned in recent years was launching me toward an unanticipated connection to the conflict in Afghanistan.

Back at home, my brave father's health took a downturn, and he had become the primary caretaker for my grandmother, who was also extremely ill.[6] The blind were leading the blind in Santa Fe, and the FBI did not have an opening in New Mexico to which I could transfer. If I stayed with the Bureau, my life would be tied to D.C. indefinitely. More and more, it seemed, the best choice I could make was to take the HTT offer.

The first week after I returned from Iraq, however, I touched down in Chicago. Janice was directing a show at the gorgeous theatre at Loyola, and she saved me the role of Carmen. It was an incredibly risky proposition for Janice—even if I made it back and arrived in time, she would have to wonder if I would be prepared—but when I would occasionally talk to her over a crackly phone connection from my base, she kindly

Janice and I backstage the night of my operatic debut in Italy.

never expressed anything but a mentor's calm confidence.

Janice is an enormous-voiced Dramatic Mezzo whose impeccable technique crafted my Lyric Contralto. This means we're both the sort of voices usually assigned to opera's most "earthy" characters, and along with this tends to come a certain personality, including a love of Carmen. Because Janice "got" me, she knew that having the role would somehow sustain me through whatever else I might have to face. I was literally still washing Iraqi sand from my hair the evening of the performance. However, when I found myself in Carmen's final confrontation with Don José on the Chicago stage, my Mom in the dressing room making sure my lipstick and earrings were big and bright enough, I realized that if I didn't return to that perfect experience—to opera—I might never truly and happily be myself.

After the *Carmen*, I went home. I stayed and helped in Santa Fe until the money from Iraq ran out. I saw my Dad and Grandmother settled in their health and care issues, and I realized what I needed to do from there. If I ever wanted to have the money to hang on to Santa Fe *and* get back to Chicago to pursue my opera studies with the earnestness that my heart continued to insist upon, I needed to take the offer to go to Afghanistan.

Because I had deployed already and returned whole, it was harder for my family to argue against it. The newness of it—as well their sense of my fragility—was gone now. Plus, the reality of my situation had again made it the most sensible option.

I was inspired by the idea that the purpose of the work would be to help commanders on the ground in Iraq and Afghanistan better understand the local culture, community-by-community, in order to avoid the unnecessary conflict that can arise out of cultural mistakes, and to offer aid better targeted to local needs. I found I cared deeply about the cultures and peoples of Iraq and Afghanistan. I had precisely the skills specified. I finally called back the recruiter, and I signed on the dotted line.

Shortly, I found myself beginning a six-month training program at Ft. Leavenworth in Kansas. A big, blonde, muscle-building six-foot-four former Marine in my class was quick to say hello and get acquainted. He boldly informed me that he was an excellent catch.

The next morning before class, he stood outside my door with a bowl of freshly made fruit salad. *The man had made me a fruit salad.* I had a personal revelatory moment.

To this point, the history of my personal relationships has been irrelevant to the story of how I arrived in Afghanistan, but here is the short version: I was not smart. I had dated and been in relationships with only a very small number of men. I had completely missed the dating games of high school because I left it so young, and I never dated in college because I was not of legal age. By the time I reached my graduate studies, my classmates and friends were generally either married or clergy.

When I did date, I had always been quick to believe promises, and to fall for words of seduction. I could never imagine "playing games" with something so important as someone's heart, so I also failed to perceive when a game was being played with mine. Somehow, no matter how badly I was hurt, I never managed to learn that lesson.

The promises I believed were always grand and empty. Never before, however, had anyone ever done something as caring and practical as making me a fruit salad. In fact, almost never had anyone made any small gesture for my sake at all. The Marine was 15 years my senior—the oldest man I ever considered dating.

I looked at the big Marine with the fruit salad and thought to myself, "Aha! I understand it all now. This is what a mature relationship looks like. It is practical and caring in small ways. I can return this with all my heart."

He had me at pineapple. We trained together, spending every day side by side. Six months later, we deployed together and planned to marry.

CHAPTER 6

Villages Without Medicines: Stomachs First

● **DAY 33**

I haven't written much lately because I'm not sure what to make of things. Patrols have become regular occurrences, but more often than not, they are disturbing. One of the first things you notice when you enter a village here is the poor health of everyone who surrounds you. While this is true in most third- and fourth-world countries—we have all seen the TV ads for Save the Children—it is uniquely disturbing in Afghanistan, because it is accompanied by a vacant and unsettled stare in the eyes of many you meet.

I wonder if this is due to illness or to a cultural/social convention that I don't yet understand. It's as if most the people—but especially the men—are looking past everyone toward something they can't quite see and are simultaneously afraid to perceive. Sometimes this stare is more resolved, and it looks like rage.

While the HTT mission is not a medical one, I think it's appropriate to act first as a sympathetic and practical person, whatever one's mission may be. It is hard to conduct a research interview on an obscure cultural topic with someone who is begging you for food or for some relief from their physical problems. This is all I find lately.

I often ask the question, "What could help your community the most?" I can't believe that stomach medicine, or sometimes specifically "Pepto-Bismol," has been my most common response from villagers.

Does the well still work? (Photo courtesy Department of Defense)

They typically suffer from gastrointestinal issues due to extremely poor sanitation and food preservation.

Before the rise of the Taliban, Pepto-Bismol, or its regional equivalent, was easily obtained from the local pharmacy. Now, no local pharmacies exist, hospitals barely exist for extreme emergencies, and Pepto is a distant memory. Everyone seems miserable.

It appears that the "trifecta" of intestinal bugs, poor sanitation, and a food supply that is contaminated in the rare instance that adequate food is available is self-perpetuating. How am I supposed to ask villages about their needs, and inspire in them any confidence in U.S. forces if I also obviously witness their suffering, and fail to help with the most glaring and easily addressed problems?

Why would villagers provide me with any information the second time we met if I did not to some degree respond to their needs after our first meeting? If the commander is going to get the "terrain" information he needs, then I needed to be able to offer the villages some gesture of reciprocity for their cooperation. Otherwise, as I can already see in the gaze of their understandably distrustful eyes, we will lose it.

● **DAY 34** Frustrated, I tromped around the camp today approaching Medical personnel, Civil Affairs personnel, and Chaplains about the issue. I scrounged around Leatherneck, trying to make friends with anyone who could get me a rucksack full of Pepto. In a strange but very real way, our mission success depended on it.

The Medical and Civil Affairs staff sincerely desired to help. However, their hands were tied. No medical supplies intended for U.S. forces can be distributed to the people of a foreign nation, and the supplies are tightly regulated. A request could be put in for a major medical aid project, and the paperwork and funding eventually approved, but there was no provision for something as simple as a pressing need for Pepto.

"Then I have a stomachache!" I burst out to the medical staff after they explained this. "Nice try," was all I got back.

I then asked my Corpsmen and Medical Officers another question. If I should find some way to magically procure Pepto that did not involve the use of U.S. supplies, would it be safe to give to Afghan villagers? For instance, could they overdose or in any other way be harmed by it? The answer was no, since Pepto was an over-the-counter product that they could simply procure for themselves, if only there were any pharmacies left. I was given the green light, if I could find my own supply.

Training along the road between Leatherneck and Bastion.
(Photo courtesy Department of Defense)

CHAPTER 7

Latrines and
Shower Scenes

● **DAY 39**

While the high temperature reached above 100 for the first time today, the latrines began overflowing. For the last two days, this event has been eminent. Those in the "know" could anticipate it from the increase of swarming flies congregating around what now hangs in the air as almost a visible, vaporous, palpable cloud of, um, the odiferous obvious.

You hesitate to breathe through your mouth, even though breathing through your nose increases your perception of the smell, because the air quality at the camp "exceeds acceptable levels for fecal content," according to the assessment of the public health officer. I am unsure what the acceptable levels for fecal content might be, but I am disconcerted to know they exist! Nevertheless, it eventually becomes unavoidable that each and every one of us, at some point, can do nothing but forge through the flies and into that fog.

The flies, of course are waiting for you when you arrive. They gather especially over the overflowing seat itself, so when you bare your bottom, they enjoy the change of cuisine and bite your sensitive "*como-se-dice*" instead.

For men there is a convenient option for certain bathroom trips, of course, when their latrines are overflowed. Newly prevalent plastic water bottles, refilled in yellow, attest to that option. ("Careful, that's not Gatorade," is the running joke of the moment.) There is no such viable alternative for women.

Always helpful, a few young and heavily tattooed Marines sharing my table at lunch offered me their favorite coping tips for entering the latrines. They beamed like fifth-graders with the sheer delight of being gross in front of a girl, and I couldn't help but love them the more for finding such cheerfulness in the circumstance.

One of their tips was to somehow acquire a bit of Vic's Vapor Rub and apply it just below your nose. Use it liberally enough, and it tends to kill your perception of anything else. They also recommended visiting the fire pit to breathe in the much "cleaner" smoke. Their third, less helpful, tip was to grow a bushy moustache. They laughed wildly, snorting on their chow, when I promised to give it my best.

I think one factor is particularly at play in the latrine problem here. Much like in the villages, intestinal bugs are unavoidable. Somehow, however, calling it an intestinal "bug" does not convey the magnitude of whatever it is that attacks your gut in Afghanistan. A bug is much too small.

The experience is tsunami-like in its proportions. It leaves the sufferer in an utterly depleted state, sometimes unable to leave the latrine for any period of time, and sometimes requiring IV fluid replacement. The latrines are not adequate for an onslaught of such seismic events.

When a toilet overflows here, it is not the same as the plumbing backing up. It simply means that the pit, which is dug below each seat and furnished with a bit of sanitizer, is spilling over. If you still have to go, you have to go, but if you were sick going in, you're going to be sicker once you get there.

The other uncomfortable issue is the lack of privacy. There are fabric partitions between the toilets, but not in front of them, so inside the women's latrine, everyone passing has a full frontal view of you attempting to look as graceful as possible with your cammies around your boots. Everyone manages the situation by wearing an unfalteringly placid expression that makes it seem they have seen nothing.

This is also the way things are handled in the women's showers, which have much the same set-up. Everyone unavoidably sees everything, but I am so impressed by the shared elegance of no one appearing to do so. Even in what could be an incredibly base and humiliating circumstance, the women manage an unblemished dignity.

Things are worse elsewhere, however. Leatherneck is big enough so that latrine issues are infrequent, and if they do occur, the equipment to solve the problem can arrive reasonably quickly and efficiently. Forward operating bases like Ramrod (I always have to giggle a bit at the masculinity of that name), and especially extremely remote combat outposts like Hotel, both of which I visited last month, do not offer such an option.

These bases have port-a-potties, which are actually convenient for gender segregation, but terribly inaccessible for maintenance when they overflow. The biggest issue with port-a-potties in the desert, though, is the occasional problem of strong and capricious winds, like those of a sandstorm. Not a few poor souls have found their facility overturned while making a visit. That, I suppose, is what might be worse than an overflow.

Also, such small and remote bases do not usually have shower facilities exclusively for women. As the furthest bastions of infantry, they would have no reason to anticipate women, and it's oddly unfortunate when you happen to be one. Luckily, prior training has taught me how to cope.

Will write more tomorrow—it's a long story.

● **DAY 40** Because of yesterday's events, I am vividly reminded of the training I underwent in the Mojave Desert before deploying. Thanks to it, I am well-prepared for what I can meet in terms of "biological," gender, and a few other challenges in Afghanistan. Actually, after that training there is very little that daunts me in the desert.

Just weeks away from deploying, our HTT training class visited the Mojave to participate in an exercise with an Army brigade, on their way out of country as well. The Mojave Desert is a wonderful place for this kind of exercise, because it truly immerses you in the stark harshness you will actually encounter. Also, the exercises are incredibly well-crafted to make you eventually lose your sense of being "home," convincing you that everything around you is a real part of the war.

As we arrived to join up with the brigade—which was in charge of all logistical arrangements—we found that women were not anticipated. Enormous tents, each housing hundreds, had been set up for the men, and these tents had heaters. Big, powerful, glorious heaters.

While the desert can certainly be hot in the day, in the early spring the nights can be as frigid and wind-blown as the land is sparse. No tent was available for the few women present. There was myself, a civilian attached to the Army (who I would meet later), a cook, and an older woman from my program we called "Mema"—a bit of affectionate Arabic for "mother." Mema is another story.

Finally, a small pop-up tent was found for us as an afterthought. Unfortunately, however, there was no provision to heat this tent. It was so tiny, heating it probably wasn't worth the logistical worry. I, with my sailor's inclinations, also wondered if the tent was actually tied down securely enough. It snapped too violently as the evening winds picked up.

A Huey and its Afghan dust. (Photo courtesy Department of Defense)

Sleeping in the tent was impossible as the temperatures dwindled toward the teens. The snapping was so loud that I got up to see if I could make it more secure. Just as I was doing so, a "bomb" hit near us (a planned explosion that was part of the exercise), and we were all required to don our helmets and run to a "hardened" location.

Of course, as the weight of the last person left the tent, my worries proved themselves worthwhile. The tent lifted off in the wind. The canvass itself remained held by one corner, but its contents blew out into the night.

I didn't know whether to run to the bomb shelter or after our things.

I saw my sleeping bag rolling swiftly away, end over end, over one dune, and most of our clothes over another. I chased them to the point of exhaustion until I simply stood atop a hill and cried mournfully after them, "Come baaaaaack!" I wasn't sure what that would accomplish, but I hoped they would obey.

The men, in their solid and warm large tents, had no such issues. In the light of day, I found my sleeping bag and some of our things. We got the tent better secured, and I went to work on the exercises.

My team at that point consisted of Pop, Lanky, Mema, and me. (Tex would later replace Mema before we left for Afghanistan.) Assigned to a certain area of operation, we went on patrols in simulated villages and interviewed actors posing as locals. We ran through various tactical scenarios. I started writing reports.

When I returned to the tent that evening, I had somewhat of a problem. Among the things that were never recovered from the desert was my stash of underwear. To this day, it doubtless still flies somewhere, freely on the wind.

When I was in the FBI, I was shocked to see that they sold employees underwear that did not require washing. Disgusted, I couldn't imagine in what circumstance that would be a good thing. Now I knew.

That evening, I hand-washed my one remaining pair of underwear. I hung it on a cable near my sleeping bag in the tent. We still had no heat, and this night was colder than the first. When I got up, I found my underwear frozen into a solid inflexible piece. I now understood why the term was "commando," but I wasn't yet ready to go so.

I was *sure* the men weren't having this problem. With an incredibly uncomfortable smile on my face, I arrived to work bright and early. The reports were going well, and we started running more serious scenarios.

We encountered angry actors. We simulated a village situation where we would have to run to a rally point. We learned how hard it really is to run distances in body armor with heavy packs.

Mema was never one for running at all. She was surprisingly senior to be in such a physically demanding program as HTT, and while she had the classically beautiful face of her Arab heritage, she was quite large. She had an endearing personality, however, that won her a great deal of slack.

She would embrace anyone, even near-strangers, with "I loooove you!," and she "loooooooooooved" my Marine in particular. Both he and I thought it nothing but sweet and motherly, because of their large difference in age.

Still, she showed me a side that made me uncomfortable. Just the week before, we were to hike a circular course in the woods near Ft. Leavenworth where we trained. She hid herself near the beginning of the path and when she thought enough time had passed, she simply walked back out. She finished with the time of an Olympian!

When an official from the program later confronted her, she wailed in hurt tears until he felt so guilty for having accused her, he gave up. She turned to me then, shockingly tearless, and said casually and disdainfully, "As if I would actually do any of these stupid things they require." I was more than a little unnerved by her lying and her "switch," so I began to put as much distance between myself and Mema as I could. We were here together now, though, and things were unavoidably close.

Just like there were no provisions for women's sleeping spaces, there were also no provisions for women's showers. (The latrines were not a gender issue, as individual port-a-potties were provided and private.) To allow us to shower, a 15-minute period early in the evening was allotted when male soldiers were instructed to stay out.

To make it in the 15-minute time slot, you literally needed to run from work, but a shower was worth it! I made it in immediately, as did the other Army contractor—a slim and pretty blonde girl who I learned went by JJ, just as I went by CC. The coincidence made us fast friends.

Because our shower stalls were adjacent with a curtain between, JJ and I struck up a conversation. She was on a different type of government-sponsored team that would interact directly with Iraqi villages, and we both wondered about how successful or safe we were going to be as females attempting the work.

"I don't know," she said, "but at least I know I can rely on my team. I'll be safe because I can count on them for anything. In fact, they're out there right now, guarding the door for us."

"That's so good to hear," I was saying mid-shampoo, precisely as a strange young man barged into the shower room. Apparently, her team had left their post.

"Female shower time!" we called out, thinking he had simply made a mistake. He kept coming.

"Get out! Females only."

The young soldier hovered too close. We did have something of a front curtain each, but they were inadequate and blowing flimsily. We could see him, probably as well as he could see us, and he was cocky. He was a bit short, with his intentionally too-tight t-shirt showing off his bulging muscles and his shorts comically too loose. He carried a towel slung over his shoulder. He supposed he was both unbearably "cool" and impressively intimidating.

He launched into a tirade as he got even closer. "You women. You're probably gonna wash that long hair, right? Take an hour to be all pretty in pink, maybe? Gonna paint your toenails? Why should you get to shower first? Why the hell do you get in here first, huh?" He snapped his towel for effect.

"What's your plan here, bastard?" I asked, cutting to the chase.

"You need to get the hell out," JJ added seriously.

Given our professional inclinations, neither one of us were girls who couldn't do at least some damage, even against such a muscular, brutish bully. All we had to do was convince him that we would give him more of a fight than he wanted, and he would back down. We both knew it. We let him feel it by showing him a confidence in our eyes that made nothing of our nakedness.

"Worthless women." He gave up and headed toward the exit, "But if I find just one long hair in the shower drain . . ." He snapped his towel again, pointlessly trying to save face in his retreat.

I smiled with some satisfaction as he turned tail, but it soon turned to outright hysterics. He ran squarely into Mema, who had only recently arrived and was just disrobing as he passed. She put more than icing on the cake.

"What?" she asked. "You never seen your Mamma?!" She revealed her copious bosom and shimmied. It all proved too much for the soldier who thought himself a "big man." He blanched and tripped on the way out the door.

While her approach was unarguably inappropriate, she did demonstrate what I ultimately thought was an important point. In our own way, each of us in the showers that day had the confidence to make our nudity a non-issue. Prudishness had no place in this environment. The self-assurance to see to your own safety was all that was worth true concern.

There was no real incident to report, though Mema enjoyed relating the funny story. Officially, a soldier had walked into the bathroom at the wrong time. Soldiers were reminded not to do so.

In the days that followed, the training became more realistic and intense. Patrols in angry villages were the norm, and as we realized that our "games" were no different from what we would actually be facing in a few weeks, any sense of "playing" faded.

During one patrol in a village that had become familiar, a sniper fired from a rooftop. At that point, everything felt real. We hit the ground. He kept firing, and soldiers were being picked off around us. I moved to better cover, and then realized that Mema could not. She lay on her belly and was breathing raggedly, crushed by her armor.

It was a game. She was basically fine. But somehow it just couldn't seem so in my mind.

It was raining death, and we couldn't find the sniper. By now I was sure there were several. They shot and ducked back into their high positions, and while we tried to maintain our cover, we couldn't see them to stop them.

Lanky was soon "dead," and Mema was a sitting duck. I grabbed her and pulled her safely with me behind a short wall—also freeing her breathing from the weight that had been stifling it. It literally took all my strength, and she was irate with me. I couldn't have cared less.

The exercise changed and we were to run again. We were to take different directions to a rendezvous point. The run was longer than I had ever done before with my armor and pack, my strength had been spent with Mema, and when I arrived at the location, my mind finally, truly, registered what we were doing.

This was real. This was very, very real. And this is what it would be like.

From the rendezvous point we moved to a central outpost, and stripping off my armor in the shade, I discovered my fiancée there. He, having found just the smallest moment and place of privacy, pulled me swiftly into his arms and kissed me. It was a life-and-death kiss, driven and heightened by the realization that too soon we would be truly at war. His team must have met snipers too, and he knew what I knew.

As he, for a last instant, lowered his head to brush his lips against my throat and I pressed close the unshaven roughness of the face that I so loved, I was startled to see the strangest intrusion. Mema, peering through a tent flap, scowled. "Go, go," I whispered to him, and wished it needed not be so as he took up his rifle and ran for his team.

Mema disappeared from work the rest of the day, and I did not see her until I entered the freezing women's tent after showering that evening. She always had a fascination with my Marine. Because of the kiss, I supposed, or because of some other offense, she would now take the opportunity—of all truly unimaginable things—to literally curse me. Her words, though they flowed from her quickly, were shockingly ornate, and crafted to a deployment. She had practiced!

"May you know the face of death a hundred times," she began, extending a hand toward me. "May tears pain your eyes always for the things that will pass. May hope meet its end in your heart, and may you never find peace all your days."

(Later, I would recount this humorously to friends as "May the fleas of a thousand camels follow always at your back, and may dung clog your boots all your days!" though I somehow always remembered Mema's shocking original words.)

She finished dramatically, pounding her heart and waving a fist heavenward, "God will hear the rage of my heart and grant this."

She was serious! I had just witnessed a bizarre superstition taken to unimaginable heights! My head rattled in confusion at her take on things right then—she had always made a point of her religious piety, and it just seemed odd to include God in a bid for such cruelty. It certainly wasn't a part of Islam as I understood it, or that I believe Muslims practiced.

"I can't imagine God would want horrible things like that," I said, trying to find some reasonable common ground, "but may He bless you and grant you peace." She really seemed to need it!

I walked out of the tent, my wet hair making me shiver violently in the wind, and found myself in tears. I didn't believe in silly curses. It was simply the fact that she had spent time working on something so florid and detailed that shocked me most. It was her hate, not her threat, that hurt.

Later that night, a good, heavy knife I was using to cut a cable and better secure our tent slipped from my grasp. Reflexively and unwisely, I caught it spinning midair, and it sliced through my hand. Two kind soldiers, a stocky lieutenant and a wiry young captain, were chewing tobacco nearby.

They happened to notice both the feat of the catch and its result. They sprung into action and came immediately to my aid. I was deeply touched.

"See?" Mema gloated as the soldiers quickly wrapped my hand and began to lead me gently away for stitches. "This deployment will go badly for you."

"Why on earth do you still insist on that?"

"See your own blood! It was not I who spilled it! Because of my prayer, God does it now!" Her voice rose disturbingly, and the soldiers traded wide-eyed looks.

Now freezing cold and badly cut, I found myself occupied trying to sort out a bit of Theology. I was fairly certain God didn't come down and slice my hand because of her prayer! Islam meant submission to the will of God, and her "curse" was an attempt not to submit to it but to bend and control it—to some very ungodly purposes.

Superstition creeps into so many religions, and this didn't appear to be Islam at all! Did she even *know* how far off she had gone from a basic tenant of her own faith? It seemed to me she did not. Of all the things that should have been bothering me at that moment, that thought, oddly, did the most.

"I couldn't possibly know," I said, "but I suspect that it's more like God's will that my hand heal up nicely. May you stay safe and whole as well." I let the soldiers lead me on then, which they did even more protectively than they had before. I get dizzy when I see a great deal of blood, and their shoulders were nice to lean on.

In the meantime, Mema sought out Lanky. She cried in her most persuasive way, and bewailed to him my cruelty toward her (for what offense, I remained unsure). Shocked, Lanky berated me the next day for upsetting an older woman, and I lacked the apparently necessary tears on call to convince him otherwise.

The whole thing was really too odd to explain anyway. Any attempt to do so would sound as strange to me as to him. I simply hoped his impression would pass if he got to know me better, but in fact, Lanky began to look at me somewhat askance afterward.

By the end of the exercise, there were all sorts of uncomfortable feelings between myself and Mema, between Lanky and myself, between Lanky and Pop, between Pop and Mema, and between Lanky and Pop and a bossy soldier from the exercise I didn't even know. Lanky, unable

On the back of a truck.

to stand any of it any longer, made a "command decision" by seizing an armored truck for the team and insisting he was driving us off the exercise grounds before anyone could order us otherwise.

Shrugging, we piled on in our dirty desert clothes with all our gear, as did anyone else we passed who was finished and wanted to get back to the main base. Lanky, however, didn't know the way quite as well as he thought he did. After an hour of long stretches and wrong turns, we found ourselves not on the trails of the exercise grounds but turning on to the main street of a tiny California town in what amounted to a tank.

Perched on top, and not quite sure what else to do, I smiled and waved to jaw-dropped onlookers like a parade queen on a float. It got more awkward when we stopped at intersections and other cars pulled up next to us, so everyone took up the friendly waving as well. "Hello, hello . . . Sorry . . . Just passing through . . . Have a nice day!"

● **DAY 43**   The office of the Chaplain has now become my favorite stop on nights before patrols—and not just for a prayer. The Navy Chaplains who accompany the Marine Corps usually have access to toiletries that kind people back in the States send for the use of the troops. Every once in a while, Chaps can provide me with that precious pink bottle, the Pepto Bismol I've been so adamant about providing to the villages.

He doesn't know many people who operate outside the wire, so in exchange for the Pepto, he's involved me in a scheme of his parish back home. Together, we've started to load my backpack with teddy bears and other cuddly toys—soft gifts for children living in a too-harsh world. Wherever I am able, he has entrusted me with getting them into the right little hands.

He doesn't know that this is a project after my own heart. In Iraq, when I couldn't sleep, I would knit teddy bears for the Iraqi children who were transported to our hospital on base for care when they were injured by terrorist or insurgent explosive devices. It happened all too frequently.

I learned to make the exact size that they could keep with them on the stretcher during the often-frightening helicopter transfers to larger hospitals, when almost everything else they had would be stripped away. At Leatherneck, however, when the sun went down, there was no light by which to knit in our shared sleeping tents. The Chaplain had the perfect solution.

● **DAY 45**   This is exciting. A huge hard-sided structure is going up—bigger than anything here. There's official confirmation: it's a going to be a chow hall. Not a field-expedient chow tent like the ones where we've been eating. It's going to be a real chow *hall*—the kinds they have on established bases, like the ones I knew in Iraq.

We've been eating "sea rats," really C-rations. They are as delicious as they sound. They are huge re-reheated re-packaged portions of whatever small pre-packaged portions might have been in an individual field ration many years ago, before M.R.E.'s were adopted.

Because they are indestructibly non-perishable, it is rumored that some date back to previous wars. They taste as if they all do. The usual fare features some version of noodles with meat.

A chow hall, though, would mean something entirely different. There would be food that was actually cooked, right there, by a real cook! Those halls make meals the highlight of your day.

Sometimes, they offer *different* meal selections at different "bars." A friendly cook might grill you a hamburger, or even make you an omelet right before your eyes! There might be pasta that was actually boiled fresh. There might be soda fountains, where you could possibly obtain a fizzy Coke.

Alright, as experience elsewhere has taught me, these chow tents are rarely staffed by Americans but by contractors from a variety of other parts of the world. Therefore, the cooks are not always familiar with the fine details of American cuisine. In Iraq, I can remember breakfast pancakes being offered with marinara sauce instead of syrup, but for the most part the chow halls were wonderful. (Besides, pancakes marinara is better than it sounds. It beats sea rats any day.)

Chow halls are so wonderful, in fact, one can lose perspective entirely. I remember how a big burly friend from my Iraq team once sat down despondently across from me at dinner and lamented, "They're out of my cran-raspberry lemonade."

"War is hell," I sympathized, and we both died laughing.

Morale at Leatherneck is at an all-time high as we watch the hall go up.

Groomed beard, darkened eyes.

CHAPTER 8

Huh? What Does It Mean?

● DAY 49

I made a mistake on patrol today that presented me with a somewhat confounding fact. I have worked long enough in Iraq and on issues of the Arab world, and have enough Arabic-speaking friends, that I've learned childlike, beginner's Arabic just to the point that it's become reflexive to answer "*Al saalam alekum*" with "*Wa alekum al saalam.*" It is as natural to the language as answering "Hello," with "Hello." All it means is "Peace be with you," and "and also with you."

However, doing so to a Pashtun man who offered me the greeting today earned me only the most confused and offended look at whatever it was that had just come out of my mouth. While Pashto speakers use the Arabic word "*Salaam*" as "Hello," because they consider it part of the Koranic tradition, no one seems to actually speak Arabic more than that one phrase. It makes me truly wonder how they understand their own sacred texts—the language of their own religion.

One important tenant of the Muslim faith is that the Arabic of the Koran is the sacred word of God, exactly as it was transmitted to the prophet Mohammed, in the precise language in which it was transmitted. If each word is the sacred speech of God, it is considered sacrilege to alter it. Therefore, translations of the Koran into languages other than the precise Arabic God spoke to Mohammed are desecrations and are strictly prohibited to the faithful.

If an average person can't answer in the simplest language of the Koran, how do they understand the Koran itself? I think to myself that a

Catholic of a previous generation would answer the liturgical phrase "*dominus vobiscum*" with "*et cum spiritu tuo*" and, despite the fact that they wouldn't speak Latin in their daily lives, would know enough to understand it basically meant "The Lord be with you," and "and also with you."

The solution, I now am reminded, is that people are taught their religion by local Mullahs, who speak the Pashto the people understand. The confounding issue is that in rural areas, Mullahs are chosen from the same villages they lead, frequently inheriting the position, or gaining it because of their prominence in the community. Typically, therefore, they don't speak or understand Arabic better than anyone else might.

If the meaning of the sacred texts, then, is never actually transmitted to the people of the faith here in southern Afghanistan, how does anyone come to truly understand the teachings of their religion except through local tradition? I wonder how often, over countless generations, local tradition might have gotten things wrong?

I remember how easily Mema seemed to have gotten her religion completely mixed up with some strange superstition—and she actually spoke Arabic herself! What could happen, then, to someone who didn't? Things foreign to a faith can sneak into it so easily. I worry about Islam when it is taken away from Arabic, and the real meaning of the Arabic isn't taught.

So many Muslims seriously educated in the Koran feel that many practices of the Muslim world (extremely drastic female mutilation in other parts of the non-Arabic speaking world, for instance) are not a part of Islam but an aberrant (and abhorrent) association of a local cultural practice to Islam. Was it even in the name of Islam at all, then, that local movements like the Taliban here imposed their extremist practices? Thinking of faithful Muslims I knew, I couldn't imagine so.

I am reminded that even when boys are educated worldwide in *madrasas*, the religious schools where they are taught the Koran, they are often taught to recite the syllables of the book by memory, like poetry. They are not taught, necessarily, to recognize what any of those syllables, so daunting and impressive to memorize, might mean as words. Instead, they are taught the beliefs of whoever might be educating them on the faith in their own language.

I worry. I truly worry. I understand more and more why it may be important for us to acquire as deep an understanding of this local culture as possible. Local culture, not Islam, may mean everything.

Putting that distressing issue out of my mind for the time being, I approached Lanky about the mistake I had made. Oddly, although we were deployed to a Pashto-speaking area, the HTT program gave us an immersion course in the other prevalent language of Afghanistan, the Dari common to the north of the country. At least more people in the Pashtun areas spoke some Dari (as opposed to almost none who spoke Arabic), so we put together a helpful review.

Lanky had an impressive talent for coming up with catchy melodies. Together, we made up a happy Sesame Street-style song to trigger our memories to the most important phrases and grammatical structures we might need to speak a bit without our translators and better establish rapport. Tex wouldn't sing along but rolled her eyes instead. The first part went:

Salaam, Salaam, Salaam alekum.
Fikir mekenoum che resish kadem.
Chittor astein? Chi al darein?
Fikir mekenoum che resish kadem.
Khoob shood marifischudem. . . .
Fikir mekenoum che resish kadem!

Hello, Hello, Hello, to you . . .
I think I might be catching a cold!
How have you been, and how's your health?
I think I might be catching a cold!
It's so very nice to meet you.
I think I might be catching a cold!

The refrain about catching a cold was not because we thought we'd often need to say it, but because it reminded us of a word pattern that was useful for saying a myriad of other basic things. Plus, it rhymed and struck us, for whatever reason, as hysterically funny. I bopped along to the song for the rest of the day.

● **DAY 50** Just before leaving work, almost at midnight tonight, I heard a ruckus in an adjoining tent and poked my head in just to see if anything was truly wrong.

"No, no . . . It just can't be like that!" exclaimed a distraught Marine master sergeant—thin, fit, and remarkably young for his rank. His haircut was the perfect length of fuzz, and I wondered how he managed to keep it precisely so. The contractors he was talking to shrugged, and looked at him with both confusion and a bit of mockery.

The Marine actually sobbed in frustration. I walked in and fiercely motioned his colleagues away as they rolled their eyes. No one has a right to mock if a Marine has a reason to cry, I thought.

"Master Sergeant, what happened here?" I tried respectfully. He held out a folded flag to me. A line of red showed where the end was tucked.

"It just can't be this way," he said through gritted teeth. "It has to be blue. It has to be *all* blue."

"Teach me. I'll be very careful, and we'll fold it the right way together."

He straightened and nodded. We unfolded the flag together and held out its corners. We measured just right to ensure that when the triangles folded, the stars were perfectly set and the seam was blue. I had met someone perhaps as obsessive as me, and we got along.

He told me about the flag as we folded. The red, he said, was for blood. If it showed on a folded flag, blood would be spilled.

"My brother deployed yesterday. My kid brother. He joined because I joined. There can't be any red." When we were done, there wasn't.

● **DAY 51** This evening, a friend from home used my last allotted moments on a crackling phone line to ask me, "So, do you enjoy killing innocent people over there?" I was too shocked and hurt to really respond, and then the connection ended. Her words cut me deeply.

She wasn't joking. Her perception was real. What would I really have said to her if I could have?

I bet she'd be confused to realize how much of the danger we face is based on attempts to avoid killing people who just might be innocent. (Mullah flashback!) I bet she'd never imagine I patrolled without a firearm, but just with my wits and my grandma's knife, so it wasn't as easy for me to kill people as arbitrarily as she seemed to imagine!

I am sure she was talking about violence in its larger sense (and the fact that I serve the goals of our military). War is not the answer, I'd tell her, and then I'd add that I just wish someone would convince the violent extremists of that fact. For whatever reasons may have led to it, at this point, they seem certain that war *is* the answer, and they're attacking innocent people.

Simply as in life, I wouldn't want to turn my back on someone clearly intent on attacking me. I'd be safer if I stood my ground and fought. Still, I'd much rather that nobody fought at all. No one longs for peace, they say, more than people actually fighting a war.

What I'm hoping to do here is help heal the situation to a degree that peace has some chance! Much like I explained to the young soldier, that's really what we're all doing as armed forces in a counterinsurgency effort. I wonder if I'm being naive by believing in the possibility of our success, but I truly do. I'm willing to bet my life on it, as is everyone here.

While I'm thinking along these lines, it reminds me of a parallel issue more specifically relevant to HTT work. I heard a similar confusion about what HTT was doing here quite frequently before deploying. The accusation was that we're "weaponizing" the tools of academic inquiry, the professional ethics of which should prohibit its use in the assistance of war efforts.

A certain part of the academic community, particularly some anthropologists, argue that such powerful tools have no place but within the walls of universities, and one certainly shouldn't exploit powerless people in war-torn countries as "human research subjects." (I laugh to picture the fact that the "research" I do on my "subjects" involves being friendly and asking simple questions about their daily lives, not some sort of horrendous human subject research, which the name itself conjures, like radical medical experimentation!)

I care about the people I research, and their lives, quite deeply. Nevertheless, I realize that there is some risk to the Afghan subjects I approach in my use of the academically-founded ethnographic and anthropological techniques in which I was trained. There is always the potential danger to them that being seen speaking to an American just might invite retaliation from the Taliban.

I mitigate this risk by conscientiously and constantly presenting the impression that I am the "annoying American" who simply barges into villages and talks to everyone whether they sought out the conversation or not—much like the survey taker at the mall. If I talk to everyone equally or seemingly arbitrarily, then it gives no impression of someone singling me out to provide information that may be to the disadvantage of the extremists.

There is a great deal of argument as to whether HTT is an intelligence effort or an academic one. To some, it seems to uncomfortably straddle the middle. HTT work isn't hidden in a "spooky" cloak-and-dagger fog of secrecy, as most people imagine intelligence must be. Its work is freely available for academic study.

There's no reason for HTT work to be secret. It's simple insight on the price of camels and kerosene and on what village needs water and why it's poor strategy to shoot a dog. Nevertheless, it seems to my conscience that this truly is intelligence and therefore falls under the ethics of that field. Without it, more lives could be needlessly lost—both Afghan and American.

I don't see myself here as an anthropologist, and I make no claims to be one. I do claim to be a well-educated researcher. Essentially, though, I see my role as a collector and analyst of intelligence on the culture of a place. There are many anthropologists in the program who feel quite the opposite. I believe we are both effective to the same end.

The essential difference, which fuels the debate, is this. Intelligence personnel are willing to accept a certain degree of risk to their human sources. It seems a fair ethical balance because the risk is most often far greater to the collectors. (Never ask someone else to do something that you wouldn't do yourself twice over, Mom always said.)

Academic efforts are unwilling to take the same risk. In this dilemma, I am compelled to make the choice most likely to give peace its best chance. I accept the risk to myself and the mitigated risk to the few to gamble for the safety of many.

Therefore, I have no compunction on the academic front, and participating in HTT seems to me an easy call. It's a matter of common sense. I would argue that if ever one's professional ethics should come in conflict with the concept of protecting the largest number of innocent lives, it may be time to rethink those professional ethics!

Sometimes the "ethical" call is not the truly moral call, much as sometimes the "legal" call is not the truly just call. (Jailhouse flashback!) War is one of those circumstances where all of these can easily conflict. In such cases, I dare say that it's easy to go with ethics and legality, but right to go with morality and justice. When push comes to shove, I want to have fought on the side of right.

If this ends up being my last diary entry, I like it.

● **DAY 56** My Pepto problem is finally solved now that a small troop store has opened on the nearby British camp called "Bastion." Bastion is a couple of miles away, but I can walk there, and sometimes I am able to hitch a ride on a colorfully decorated Afghan truck. Passing drivers will give you a lift, but only if you can run and jump on the flat truck bed. They wave and toot a friendly goodbye when you jump off.

I now buy out the stock whenever the store has a shipment of stomach medicine. (Our own troops, and the Brits, have plenty of access to Pepto through their official medical supplies.) Finally, I can return to the nearby villages able to demonstrate to my interview subjects that I respond to their needs and am interested in building a relationship—not just exploiting them for information.

It is only now, after beginning to share bottles of Pepto, that I have begun to understand the look in the eyes of the villagers. They are sick, uncomfortable, unhappy, and there is no modern medical aid available to them. It seems that the medicine they use, with apparent frequency, is whatever comes from grandma's kitchen, and from the opium poppies and wild marijuana trees that grow in abundance wherever one looks.

I've been asking around about this. Older women tell me if that if a child is teething and inconsolable, why not soothe the baby with a bit of gum from the poppy? If your stomach hurts, why not do the same? It was only a few generations ago that this would have been considered valid medical advice in the U.S.—our medicines consisted of drugs that we now consider illegal, and harmful as well. It would be hard for any adult raised from infancy with this kind of medical "care" not to suffer some damage or dependency, and drug addiction appears widespread beyond anyone's capabilities to estimate.

DAY 57 The only thing interesting about the patrol today was a straggly black goat in a tree. What passes for a tree here is really more of a large dead bush with some thin extending branches. That's what makes it surprising that the goat was there. He was standing with all four hooves balanced on the end of what was essentially a twig, holding him hovering just off the ground. I wasn't sure what he had accomplished by managing the feat.

I've met goats before. They're rambunctious and curious. This one offered only a deadpan stare and an angry "Blaaaanh."

"Hi, Goat."

"Blaaaaaaaanh."

"Okay, okay. Sorry!"

"Blaaaaaaaaaaaaanh!"

I gave him a wide berth as I walked past his "tree."

Even the goats here seem different in a way I just don't understand. Everything still feels like a strange planet, and I can't yet quite find a key to translation—even with a goat! How will I ever find that translation with the people, as I've been tasked to do? I console myself with the thought that articulating my confusion is the first step in sorting it all out.

DAY 60 I am still trying to work out the drug dependency issue I have begun to observe. I'm not sure that medical issues are the only factors at play in this phenomenon, but I can't understand what else there might be. Much earlier, in Kandahar, I met trainers of Afghan military and police forces, who interact on an almost constant basis with young local men. They spoke of drug issues too, but I didn't record our brief and casual conversation. That's always a mistake.

Yesterday I sought to remedy my error and gather some greater detail by interviewing another one of these trainers. Fortunately, I met one at lunch last week. (As HTT training taught me, it usually pays to be chatty.) He was an officer among the few Army personnel (as opposed to Marines or civilians) walking around Leatherneck lately, so he was easy to spot, and he was happy to oblige after a small bribe of the "good" energy drink—the blue one—that is only occasionally in the chow halls. Everyone hoards it and then uses it for barter.

He began by expressing his affection for the young men he trains and

Conference after harvesting wheat.

his hopes that they will be able to take on the security challenges of Afghanistan's future. After the energy drink, however, he started to express his doubts that they could do it. He worried about his trainees' tendency to want to "block out the world," and to "avoid obvious reality"—a dangerous leaning when weapons training is involved, so he had become extremely aware of this oddly prevalent trait.

He then told me a story of the time he provided a brand new government-funded truck for the use of a just-graduated class of Afghan policeman. Not long after, he also provided the young men with a box of metallic stickers featuring the Afghan flag. These were part of a campaign to build a sense of national awareness and identity among Pashtun children—a necessary development if Afghanistan is ever to function under a sovereign government instead of in two halves, with the southern half effectively ungoverned by anything but tribal rule.

The police were to distribute the flags to children they encountered, thereby beginning to build a friendly relationship with the community, as well as teaching an important point regarding nationalism. Instead, the young men returned the next day with their truck "decorated." Afghans love to decorate their trucks, and vehicles are often brightly painted with beautiful designs on the sides and furnished with pretty curtains and tassels around the edges of the windows.

The young policemen, however, had done something entirely different. They had covered every inch of clear glass on the truck with the flag stickers—the front windshield included. They couldn't see to drive, but were unbothered by the fact as they rolled down the road, the driver relying on the guidance of the men that rode in the truck bed. The trainer did not mention drug use specifically, but he pointed out that their desire not to see, or to "block out the world," to use his words, had been taken to an extreme.

This led me back to many earlier field notes I reviewed today. Often, the commander wanted to know who the inhabitants of certain villages went to in case of trouble. It was a question I asked often. We always hoped the answer would be U.S. forces or, even better, local government authorities.

While the answers varied, they consistently conveyed that people felt they could not go to the police, who they viewed as notorious for being nearly constantly intoxicated on marijuana or opium and not caring about the needs of the community. People frequently characterized the police as living together in their stations and not dealing much with the world outside—except on the occasions that corrupt officers stole from the villagers. One interviewee in my notes accused the police of being more interested in the young serving boys they kept at their stations than in anyone else in the community.

If I were to summarize the general local sentiment, it appeared that the police saw their position as one of privilege in the community, evidenced and reinforced by their weapons and authority, which entitled them to take what they wanted. Perhaps this meant they viewed those of lesser station as "servants." I wasn't sure.

While I met some truly heroic Afghan policemen, this general distrust of the police was one of the most compelling reasons for villages to look to the Taliban for some hope of assistance and rough justice. The best Afghan policemen were aware of this problem and did their utmost to combat it. Nevertheless, the situation was utterly disheartening.

The information on the police—recruited from local young men—was somewhat helpful in understanding the greater picture of the drug problem, but ultimately, of course, it was not only the police who bore the appearance of frequent drug use. Most young men appeared troubled, and no wonder. Few positive prospects existed for their future.

It seems illogical that there could be a further shared cause for the problem of drug dependency and/or reality avoidance that affects so much of Afghanistan other than the natural availability of drugs and the misery of poverty, since such a cause would have to be equally widespread. Still, it nags me that something else must certainly be at play to create such an extreme dependency. I have now spent days running in a research circle that has led me nowhere except to more questions.

No report will come of this, so I am going to chow. By the way, when is that big chow hall going to open? We're still eating in the miserable little field tents.

CHAPTER 9

Boots Don't Bend

● **DAY 67**

Boots don't bend. I found today this was a critically important point that no one has considered except, of course, the people who suffer from the issue. However, they can't do much about the boots.

Today, I accompanied a Marine patrol, and we encountered a few young men lounging around a dirt-bike repair shop. The day was already hot, and they had no business, so they sat, smoking and talking. Seeing them, it was only appropriate to take a moment, say hello, and ask them a bit about their local circumstances.

I didn't get the feeling that they necessarily liked us, but they were obliging. One of the men ducked inside to bring everyone some tea. They invited us to sit with them in their circle in front of their shop and served us.

The problem is this: the men in these rural areas rarely sit on chairs. Instead, from the time they are children, they sit balanced above the ground, their legs bent in front of them and their weight resting on their heels. They are so comfortable in this position, and their requisite muscles are so strong and accustomed, that they will sit and chat for hours like this without giving it a second thought.

To sit otherwise is to appear very "off." To stand when you are invited to sit and join conversation is to appear very rude. To sit with your rear on the ground is to appear embarrassingly dirty. The only way to avoid all of this, then, is to attempt adopting the hovering, weight-on-your-heels position.

The conversation was sparse. The young men were just as polite as necessary, and answered my questions—where they were from, how was business (with the actual curiosity whether many people owned dirt bikes nearby), and what they felt was most needed in their area. Basically, we just attempted to offer a friendly hello and let them know we were around to be helpful.

We finished our tea. We tried to rise to leave. We failed.

"Okay, well, goodbye!" We tried to extend the conversation while we wondered how to get ourselves up.

"Alright, goodbye, then . . ."

"It's been nice talking to you . . ."

"Yes, very nice . . ."

"See you again sometime . . ."

"Um, certainly . . ."

This went on interminably. Our problem was that our boots didn't bend. In order to balance on your heels, your toes have to flex to touch the ground. Ours wouldn't, until that painful moment when, under the complete weight of body, armor, and pack, the top leather finally "snapped" into a sharp crease, cutting our feet just above the instep.

Then our feet were basically trapped and painfully immobile, but that wasn't the whole problem. The small muscles of our legs, along with our knees, were the mechanism needed to lift not only our bodies but the crushing weight of our gear off from the crouched position. After we made our first attempt, it occurred to us that this wasn't easily accomplished, and we needed to devise some alternate strategy.

Unfortunately, all of our alternate strategies involved something like waddling, tipping ourselves to one side, falling forward onto our knees, or just reaching out a hand to one of our colleagues who had already managed to stand.

Of course, at that point, our legs and feet were either in pain too excruciating to walk or completely asleep, so we still needed to find some excuse to stay put while we allowed those issues to resolve. We said goodbye one unbearably unnecessary last time. We smiled broad confident smiles and finally walked away with all the dignity we could muster.

CHAPTER 10

". . . Too Damn Cruel"

● DAY 70

I backtracked to the sleeping tent today because I had forgotten a notebook there that I needed in the work tent. It's bizarre, but the idea of walking back to the sleeping tent in the middle of the day is far more intimidating than it sounds. It's almost a 20-minute challenge each way, not so much because of the distance but because of the heat. With no shade between the tents, the new high of 117 degrees outside is so extreme it immediately drains you of any physical strength. (This is why we patrol only in the mornings or evenings.)

One must prepare for such a journey, and almost needs a firm handshake from colleagues before setting off. First, it is important to drink a bottle of water. Second, it is important to take a bottle of water. Third, it is important to plan out an ideal pacing. If you start out too fast because you don't initially feel the full effect of the heat, you'll suddenly find yourself too exhausted to continue in the middle.

If you do this and faint, you'll probably not live down the teasing for a long while. If you're female and you faint, you'll likely be labeled as too weak to belong here. However, if you walk slowly enough to avoid the burn-out, but fast enough to get out of the sun quickly, you'll be fine. It's an art.

Feeling happily accomplished for having managed all of the above, I was surprised to find another woman in the sleeping tent when I walked in. I didn't know her, but I hardly knew any of the women who shared the tent. My work schedule meant that I usually arrived just as the lights were out and quiet was expected, so lately I rarely talked with or even saw most of them. They often knew one another from working together, but I wasn't a part of any of their teams.

It appeared she was hurriedly packing her gear. Everyone was still just arriving at the camp in recent months, so it seemed an unusual time for anyone to be leaving. She turned to me suddenly, her eyes filled unexpectedly with tears and anger.

"Have you seen a hairbrush?" she asked agitatedly. "It was my good one, from a salon."

"I'm sorry, no."

"See?" she fumed, "That's the way it is around here. They take what they want, regardless of what it might have cost me. It's completely f*cked up—it's too damn cruel!" She gasped and turned away.

It promptly occurred to me that we weren't talking about a hairbrush anymore, but that's all we would say, just then, about her rape.

"Okay, honey, now you listen to me," I said, shaking her just a bit out of her tears. "Your hair is gorgeous, and it has not a damn thing to do with that brush." I lifted her hair a bit out of her eyes. "The brush doesn't matter one little bit. You're beautiful, regardless of the heartless things other people might do. Those things matter nothing. Nothing. They can't take anything away from your real beauty. They can steal from you, but they can take nothing away from you. You understand that?"

"The bastard. That f*cking bastard," she cried.

"I know, sweetie, I know." As I sat with her, I wondered how it happened. Perhaps he hit her over the head, and she never saw it coming. Perhaps she did see him first, though. I thought about how the ladies in the shower and I once faced down our potential attacker and won. That's often what it took, I thought, to keep from getting hurt.

But how, just how, was she supposed to know that? From her soft eyes and gentle round face, I wondered how she would pull off the stupid confidence game, even if she knew. Her eyes would harden now, I was certain.

"I think I ought to just have my hair cut short," she finally sniffed and sighed.

"No, sweetie, you wear it long and defiantly."

I thought to pull her hair up gently into the Marine bun she was too shaken to make herself, without her brush, but she suddenly and wordlessly stormed from the tent. By evening, her things were gone. I never saw her again.

Nothing was acknowledged, perhaps because she herself had requested it be kept quiet. I doubted many people knew her any more than I did or noticed her presence missing. Suddenly, however, word went around camp to be especially cautious when alone in the dark.

Lanky took Tex and me aside to inform us that he'd had a "special talk" with the Commander, and that she and I were to walk only together at night. I'm still not sure how two women are safer together than they would be with a man. They might just be a bigger target, but Lanky wasn't offering to walk with us himself.

At this point, I'm getting beyond the expectation (if not the hope) that help or security will come from anyone else. I remember fondly the two soldiers who rushed to my aid when I cut my hand, but I've learned in general that you can't bet anything on "waiting for the cavalry," and you're safe only when you have your own wits about you. It's sad, but it's old news now, and it's better to know than not.

This evening I started walking with Tex. We walked all the way to the store at Camp Bastion. We bought little flashlights and speculated. We trusted Marines. We trusted them implicitly.

Still, our camp was truly nothing but thousands of strangers in this wild isolation. We have started to see building contractors and food workers and laundry workers and sanitation workers and who knows who else from all over the world. It was frightening. Among the thousands, there could even be a single Marine gone wrong, and it was so profoundly dark at night.

On the way, we were surprised that we both found sentimental the same old songs in Spanish. One speaks to the ghost of a weeping woman —La Llorona—a favorite fixture of Hispanic folklore. It reminded me of home, but the melancholy melody was haunting on the desert wind.

Dicen que no tengo duelo, Llorona,
Porque no me ven llorar.
Dicen que no tengo duelo, Llorona,
Porque no me ven llorar.
Hay muertos que no hacen ruido, Llorona,
Y es mas grande su pena.

They say that I have no sorrow, *Llorona*,
Because they don't see me cry.
They say that I have no sorrow, *Llorona*,
Because they don't see me cry.
But there are the dead who are silent, *Llorona*,
And for that they suffer the greater.

We sang together as we walked the dusty road and watched the sun set. I kept the hairbrush drama to myself, but I hope that woman finds her peace. I hope she keeps her hair long.

● **DAY 71** After yesterday's encounter, I've started to be more aware of ladies in the tent. I don't want to fail someone by missing the fact that they need help if they do. It was by sheer coincidence that I found that woman yesterday. I should pay more attention to the people close by.

Something consistent strikes me about them. For the most part, they're pretty in a way I'll never be. They are thin and tall and typically all-American blue-eyed blondes. They are the kinds of girls, I imagine, who would have both made cheerleader and captained the chess team—smart and accomplished with a continual expectation of success. It's interesting to me to see the makings of Marine officers.

There's not much interaction to be had. It's still true that my schedule is different than others, so I don't get back to the tent early enough at night to spend much time with the ladies before the lights go out, nor do I share their schedule in the morning. It's also true that I'm not one of their own.

They're polite. So am I. Women Marines. "Even Fewer, Even Prouder," I think to myself with a smile. They earned it.

There are harsh differences that seem to keep us separate, although our goals are so much the same. Most are required to carry their M-16 rifles everywhere. To them it is a symbol of pride, of Marine-hood. No rifle rattles in when I enter the tent, so I lack that badge.

I, however, without a rifle or the well-earned pride of a Marine, am required to go into dangers that they are not allowed. With their rifles, these are the dangers they long to face. I seem to be unforgivable on both counts. To some degree, I understand.

Looking around, I've noticed that as neatly as the bunks are made, nobody is ashamed to have a teddy bear perched on top. We all certainly need a little comfort. It makes me wonder about the men's tents. Was anyone hiding a teddy bear there? ("Um, it's from my girlfriend," I could just imagine a teenage Marine trying to explain in his best baritone.)

I have a little stuffed lion from my Mom. At least he's a trusted friend. He loyally stowed away in my luggage when I spent long and lonely months on recital tours. Mom chose a lion for courage, so I named him, aptly, Couraggio.

"*Couraggio!*" Nanu would always say. It was advice, encouragement, and admonishment combined. "*Couraggio!*" he insisted on in everyone, if nothing else. It was a family motto.

No rifle, but little Couraggio. He, a rosary, and a knife are what lie next to me at night. Each is its own comfort.

CHAPTER 11

"If They Are Stronger, It Is Theirs for Them to Take"

● DAY 76

Much like before, we have accomplished what was possible out of Leatherneck for the time being. Enough patrols have gone out into the surrounding areas that the neighbors are familiar with the Marines, we are thoroughly familiar with important villages for great distances, and the commander feels that is adequate for now. There is no work for us and, far worse, the chow hall has not opened.

So the commander has sent us off to assist the British forces with which the Marines are now working closely. The Brits have bravely held surprisingly large areas of southern Afghanistan with incredibly small numbers of troops. Now that the Marines will be taking over some of those areas, everyone wants the transition to be smooth.

Naturally, the British commander at Lashkar Gah has his own patrols going out to the more rural areas, and information that we can gather will be of use both to the Brits and the Marines. That's the plan, at least. Right now, all that has happened is that we have made plans with the commander and shuttled back and forth to Leatherneck trying to retrieve our gear.

Catching a helicopter to wherever you might be trying to go is a fascinating art here. There are flight schedules, but they change so regularly (due to the chaos of the obviously intervening war) that they're almost not worth anyone writing down. You can run to the helopad at a supposedly scheduled time, and occasionally you will see a helicopter. If you do, it is very likely that this helicopter will keep on flying by while you jump and yell frantically from the ground.

According to the "schedule," if this happens to you, the next possible flight will be days away. The only real solution, we have learned as a team, is to sleep on the helopad. Not on it, necessarily, but right next to it. I purchased a nice new British sleeping bag—much lighter than the American issue and a much prettier green—precisely for this purpose.

Tiny triumphs.

When you hear any helicopter coming, you wave and beg to get on if it is going in remotely the direction you are headed. I have learned this is easiest if you are female and smile broadly. You charge into the rush of the propeller blades while the air is sucked powerfully from your lungs and the blowing sand shreds your skin and clothing. If you make it through, you jump on.

Your sand-blasted self then gets completely covered in the greasy lubricant that drips from most parts of the craft's interior. (Incidentally, this is the *real* reason everyone wears camouflage in a war zone. It's the only fabric that still looks presentable when it's covered in stains.) You repeat this process until you ultimately reach your destination. You retrieve your gear, and you then begin the adventure of attempting a return.

I think this process has finally reached its conclusion as of yesterday. I now have enough gear between Leatherneck, Lash, and Kandahar, that I should be able to move between the three locations without much trouble. It seems I am usually required to do so lately.

I am surprised to find that my "team" works as a team quite rarely. We are often separated, which only makes sense given the area we try to cover. However, when we are together at one location, I still find that I am typically assigned to patrols and execute the team's research plans and reports on my own.

My team leader says he has delegated me these tasks because I "like writing papers." I don't believe anyone actually likes writing papers, and I've told him so, but I want to fulfill my role the best I can. I do wish we worked together more closely. I like the feeling of having a team, and I miss it when it's not there.

We are together for the time being, even though it may be weeks more before our first planned patrols with the Brits, and I will be sent to Kandahar and Leatherneck again in the intervening time. Today, it was my turn to attend the early morning briefing here in Lash. I sat respectfully among the tiny group gathered.

The British commander is an exceptionally proper, intelligent, and kind officer. He grasped on the value of HTT work right away and has spent hours talking to us and planning with our team. He was the perfect model of military formality until today.

The commander looked down to collect his thoughts before the briefing, and suddenly became unable to suppress a laugh. He finally snorted out loud and managed to say "bitty little boots" between gasps. He then turned pink with laughter.

"I'm sorry, it's just that CC's got those bitty little boots. I've never seen combat boots so tiny. I didn't know the Americans made them. I guess they have to if they send bitty little CC."

"Sorry CC," he added, clearing his throat, suddenly contrite, formal, and very British once again. That sent me into fits of laughter. The meeting was dismissed.

● **DAY 83**   Today, a schoolteacher—the only one I have yet met in Afghanistan—gave me what I know will be one of my most lasting and treasured memories. He was a kindly and humorous older gentleman with a severely malformed eye that had never been repaired. He joked that the disfigurement always allowed him to keep one eye on his class.

He brought out his students to greet us as we walked to observe a local *shura*, or community meeting. A functioning and integrated class was an extreme rarity. Anticipating our arrival, he had taught them, girls and boys alike, to recite and write out a message in English: "Welcome to our home."

One boy, with a brand new pen, wrote his best English in my diary for me, so I could keep the words:

The teacher then took me aside and asked me to please remember his class's sincerity in this sentiment, especially when I encountered villages that felt otherwise.

I am reminded that on almost every patrol lately, we are besieged with groups of children. Afghan children know well not to fear Western forces, but to view them as potential sources of treats, gifts, and candy. The way the children behave when they do this, however, is as widely varied as are the attitudes of their individual villages.

There are times when the children of a village will approach the patrol with twinkling eyes and smiling, gentle faces. They remind me of the class we met. These children don't ask for treats, but simply greet us with "*Salaam!*" and happy waves while they march and run along beside us.

When we, with melted hearts, dig in our pockets for gifts, they receive them gratefully and share them without fighting. Girls in these groups receive gifts equally with boys. These are always the same villages in which we find adults fiercely opposed to the Taliban and working with great determination to build their own future.

However, the schoolteacher was right about the contrast we would encounter as villages greeted us with the opposite of his class's welcoming message. Other groups of children could be as frightening as the villages from which they came. They would mob the patrol with demands, and if they believed they did not receive everything that you might have, the boys would grab at you and attempt to dig in your pockets. You could hear these groups of children approach from a distance, because they would yell for pens and candy. Their fierce shouts of "*Qalaam!*"—a demand for a pen—became almost a battle cry.

Being mobbed by these children—"the *Qualaam* kids"—often posed dangerous tactical issues. More frequently than I care to remember, our patrols would become penned in in narrow streets or alleys by two large groups of demanding children on either side. Narrow passageways are called "gateways of death," because it is so easy for even a large patrol to be trapped and killed by a small number of enemies in that unique situation.

It was a gut-twisting circumstance, because we didn't want the mob of children hurt if someone should open fire upon us from above or from a side door, and we knew we couldn't fight our way out of the trap with children hemming us in on either side. The Taliban had no problem risking and sacrificing young lives for its cause, so an enemy sniper would have no compunction about firing on us, even surrounded by children, from the walls above.

We were "easy pickings" in this situation—trapped by the angry children that we wouldn't harm to escape. I knew what was possible. I vividly remembered our training for snipers in the Mojave, and I was horrified. It seemed by sheer miraculous intervention that a massacre hadn't happened yet. Each time we were again trapped, the odds increased against us.

At night, when someone in the tent would wake up suddenly shaking from a nightmare, we would tease them that it was not gunfire or explosions they were dreaming about—they must have been dreaming that they were being chased for a pen. It has become a running joke around base to startle each other with outbursts of *"Qalaam!,"* as if this is the most frightening exclamation one could imagine. In a certain way, it is.

The behavior of the demanding children, besides being disturbing, is revealing in many ways. When faced with these groups, it is essential to have exactly enough gifts for each child to receive one. Otherwise, it is safer to give nothing. If one child is perceived to have gotten more than another, a fight will break out, which will quickly turn into a violent free-for-all until the stronger boys have everything or until the gifts—usually pens or notebooks—are destroyed in the fighting.

In these groups, one would notice that the girls do not join in with the boys, but hang back if they are seen at all. If a gift is given to a girl, it will immediately be taken away by the boys. There is a danger that she may even be hurt for the offense of having it.

At the home of one large family I visit or pass by with some frequency, there is a girl of about nine or ten who watches me with a certain curiosity. Unlike her brothers, who are usually part of the angry mobs, she is gentle and inquisitive. I could tell she was fascinated by my watch—which was oddly pink and frilly for military attire.[7] Last week, away from the mob and in the sight of her parents, I gave her the watch, thinking this would ensure she would be allowed to keep it and perhaps retain a pleasant memory of an American when she grew older.

● **DAY 86** Just today I saw the oldest brother of the young girl I befriended. As usual, he was leading an angry mob of children, but waving a fist adorned with the pink frilly watch. I borrowed a translator and stopped him.

"Hey! That's your sister's watch."

"It's mine now. She gave it to me."

"Did you take it from her?"

"I would have if she hadn't given it to me, but she knows better."

"Can you tell the time? I showed your sister how."

"No, I like the way it looks."

"But everyone can see that watch is meant for a girl. It's a pretty bracelet. You're a big strong boy. Aren't you ashamed to wear girls' things?"

"I can wear girls' things all I want! I can take girls' things and I can like them!"

The conversation left me surprised. I erroneously thought I could shame the boy into returning his sister's watch by pointing out the gender-confusion issue, but it didn't faze him. In fact, he seemed quite proud to like wearing girl's things. At the same time, he was also proud of his ability to dominate a girl with threatened or actual violence.

More interestingly, he was the boy whose behavior appeared to be emulated by the peer group he led, as they nodded along in agreement with him when he spoke defiantly to me and the translator, then resumed their "*Qalaam!*" chant at his urging. Therefore, none of the other children seemed to think his penchant for obviously feminine apparel was unusual or a cause for any teasing or ostracization, as it most certainly would have been in America. Instead, they idolized him.

The attitudes of children, of course, are formed by the adults around them. I found many similar patterns involving the deprivation of women and the automatic usurping of whatever might be theirs in the homes of adults and community leaders with whom I visited. While the children wanted treats, the adults were at times equally demanding of food, fuel, and other resources. I was always disturbed to see households of malnourished women, sometimes too weak to even stand in the summer heat, headed by portly and apparently vigorous men.

The men who were successful enough to marry in Pashtun society sometimes married more than one woman, and almost always had astonishing numbers of children. The challenge of keeping them fed was daunting, and women, because of both physical and social issues, were the most deprived. The malnutrition issue was beginning to come to the forefront of my awareness—much like the Battle of Pepto Bismol had a bit earlier.

● DAY 90 "Stop them! I have plenty of gifts for them, but that is especially for your youngest daughter, who needs it. If she doesn't eat more iron, she will only get weaker."

The girl, not quite in her teens, looked confused as her own sisters took the food and medicine from her hands. Then she slipped into a more resigned weakness. I thought she might faint in the heat.

Her father responded flippantly to my insistence. "If they are stronger, it is theirs for them to take." I could not help but be reminded of the behavior of the children in the mobs, who in their desperation to be the strongest, destroyed what they could have had.

● **DAY 91**   With that father's casual cruelty carved into my mind, I find myself alone, crying with rage. I am again attempting to sort out my thoughts through re-examining field experiences. I plan to rant here for a while, as I have an entire weekend to write. I am not planning on, nor capable of, moving a single inch.

The temperature, here in the shade of my tent, is 115 degrees. Power is out thanks to what air conditioning there was blowing all the circuits in Lash. In case you might want to take a "shower" (really a short burst of cold water), what little water supply we had has been out for three days. The latrines are backing up.

The unmistakable aroma of hot humanity sits thickly in the air, and despite the temperature, I am tempted to wrap a shawl fashionably around my face, just to cover my nose and mouth. I am too exhausted from the heat to go anywhere, and too bothered on several fronts to do anything but sit here and think. I am literally and figuratively steamed.

Many of my visits to villages have begun to show me the reality of the lives of women and children in relation to the lives of men. I am stunned as I start to see the truth of which members of the family get whatever resources are available, and the effort that people are and are not willing to put forward in order to improve their own situation when the opportunity is presented to them.

While men occasionally share a goat with each other at their community meetings or "*shuras,*" at which women almost never participate, most women I meet in the extremely rural areas receive very little protein or iron. It seems that once a young girl begins her period and is relegated completely to a woman's world, she is almost permanently doomed to physical problems. The girls that confide to me that they have particularly long and heavy periods suffer from obvious anemia, and the women whose bodies are taxed by almost constant pregnancy suffer worst of all.

Again, it's hard to visit these women and establish friendships without offering some simple gestures of help, but the same restrictions that apply to the distribution of medicines also apply to food. No regulation can

A Qalaam boy.

stop me, however, from developing a hoarding tendency for the bags of beef jerky and packets of peanut butter that are served in the chow tents, or from stashing away my M.R.E.'s to share later. These are the best sources of protein, iron, and calories I can find. The copious pockets of my uniform bulge after I leave the chow tent on days I have patrols, and the female translator with whom I work has quickly picked up the same habit.

A small gift from a visiting American is no solution to the long-term problem of malnutrition, however. We sometimes go on missions to assess what self-sustaining community projects could be put into place, backed by U.S. or British funding. Instead of simply giving food that will shortly run out—especially when NATO forces eventually leave Afghan-istan—we want to show villagers there are ways that they can produce their own food and income, without having to rely on international forces or the Taliban. They can support their families and end their suffering on their own.

Particularly exciting to me are the funds available to commanders for micro-grants which would enable families, even women, to receive the start-up costs and materials needed to establish their own small busi-nesses. I have tried explaining all sorts of agricultural options to local farmers, from being provided instruction and set-up in drip irrigation techniques, which are low-cost and work wonderfully in arid environ-ments, to small livestock business options, where chickens would be pro-vided so families could eat and sell the eggs.

I see these things as real solutions to the cycle of poverty and anger which lends power to extremists and terrorists. I had been confident that the villagers—who, like the children yelling *"Qalaam,"* constantly insisted on their need for more assistance—would be thrilled. Instead, I began to have my almost indomitably optimistic heart broken.

Slowly, patrol after patrol, while often conducting surveys on labor and agriculture, I have found that most men who define their profession as "farmer" do little farm work at all. Blaming political unrest and a poor climate, they do not plant their fields. If they do plant, it is not with a food crop but rather a crop of poppies, the sale of which inevitably aids the Taliban and al Qa'ida.

Tending of the fields and any food-producing gardens within their compounds is women's work and belongs to their wives. Many "farmers" I have met spend most of their days gathered together with the men and boys of the village, enjoying one another's company by having discus-sions, smoking, and playing games—sometimes even leaving the village together for walks in the desert or treks to procure sparse flowers for one another. The men have a gentle and leisurely refinement—but one that seems so out of place in the context of the suffering around them.

While their wives remain at home, poorly groomed and dressed in the most conservative clothes imaginable, many farmers, like the boy with the pink bracelet, are comfortable adorning themselves as elaborately as possible, some even enjoying eye makeup and henna-painted hands. As evidenced by their clearly non-work-oriented attire, most of these "farmers" are completely uninterested in a small business that would entail more farm work, like raising chickens or tending string irrigation systems.

Somehow, however, these men were also extremely unwilling to allow their wives, who would clearly end up doing the actual work, to participate in the programs. Though they tend not to explain their reasoning, my personal guess is that it is for fear that the women might begin to feel empowered—as if they could accomplish something for their families that their husbands could not. Instead, the farmers argue and become increasingly angry in their insistence that it is the responsibility of the government —either the government of Afghanistan or the governments of Western countries—to provide entirely for food and the complete sustainment of their communities.

Because no government has adequately done this so far, their dissatisfaction and anger only increases. As I sat in on one *shura* and observed the discussions, I heard the heartbreaking declaration, "If you can give us chickens for eggs, you can give us chickens to eat. If we have chickens, we will eat them. Then you will give us more."

I was gloomily reminded of Paula and her apricot orchard. I was also dismayed as to where this vehemently held idea of complete dependence on the state had come, as the Pashtun people had for centuries been proudly independent and had no experience of ever being provided for in this way by any government.

I must consider, though, that some Pashtun communities display the absolute opposite of this tendency. I remember a group of families I encountered along the roadside, together thrashing grain on some particularly colorful oriental carpets. The girls played with the boys as the men and women worked together to feed their families, and the children were friendly and clearly happy. The small group did not have much of a harvest, but what they did have, they planned to share as a community in the truest and noblest tradition of Pashtunwali—the tribal code of honor that has guided the Pashtun people since time immemorial.

When I stopped to visit with this little band, they asked me where my patrol was going. I explained we were headed to the next village, about two miles further along the road. They were actually shocked by the idea of going so far. "We never go over there. The people are so *different* there."

I began to understand how right they were. In southern Afghanistan, the cultural and attitudinal differences between two locations can be vast, even separated by a short walk. This is the challenge of understanding the "Human Terrain" of this area—no overall assessment can apply to any individual village, and only in-person research, on the ground, can begin to reveal the truth about each community.

Even in an "angry" village, one family loved the idea of a micro-grant. I was taken by the intricate beauty of two teenage girls' needlework, and I asked if they ever sold their work or provided it to friends. "We wish we could! Imagine what beautiful things we could design and make for everyone's weddings! However, we can't afford thread anymore, we can't get to the bazaar we used to go to because of the Taliban roadblocks, and there isn't much linen left there anyway. We haven't embroidered for months!"

When I explained that a micro-grant could fund their business idea, and that our commander was even willing to look into ways that we could deliver them a shipment of linen and thread while it was still difficult for them to obtain, I saw light and empowerment in the girls eyes, and nothing but beaming pride in their father's. My badly wounded optimism has moments like this when it begins to heal. I have begun to think that one difference in the life of a family still makes our work worthwhile, even if the social problems at large do feel overwhelming.

CHAPTER **12**

We Spell Misery
M.R.E.

● **DAY 92**

We went nowhere today, but we ate plenty. We started to go somewhere, but the truck we were in broke down. That's never a fun situation, because as you wait in the desert while another vehicle goes to request a repair, you realize you are nothing but a sitting duck, should the enemy happen to find you.

We livened up the long hour by sharing our M.R.E.'s with our British counterparts while we waited. They had heard much about the American M.R.E—the indestructible individual field ration ubiquitous to modern warfare. I shared with them that the oddly backwards acronym stands for "Meal, Ready-to-Eat," but due to its typical impact on one's digestive system, it is usually referred to by Marines here as "Meal Refusing to Exit."

Much of what is thought about M.R.E.'s is generally untrue. First of all, we do have something resembling "real" food here. We'll have great food as soon as that chow hall in Leatherneck opens. (What's going on with that, anyway?) M.R.E.'s are only for those times when chow happens to be otherwise inaccessible.

We take them on patrols with us. We eat them when we're working too far away from a chow tent or on something too involved to make the trip worthwhile. We eat them when we are camped waiting for a helicopter or when facilities aren't functioning or when we've *really* had it with chow tent's offerings. Mostly, we sneak them to hungry villagers.

M.R.E.'s are not all bad. Generally, they're just not good. I do have a particular liking for the one labeled "Vegetable Omelette." People tend to leave this one alone, so I get my favorite almost every time. It consists of a highly condensed patty of egg, which reminds me in flavor of something like a quiche or a frittata or a Spanish tortilla—especially when combined with the occasionally-cooked potatoes, also conveniently included in the pack. There is usually an additional side of nacho cheese-filled pretzel bites.

The Vegetable Omelette selection also includes a small packet of hot apple cider mix. I am not sure why someone would want hot apple cider while enjoying an omelette and pretzels in the desert. However, I have

Cheerful and a Huey.

found that the packet makes a very nice dessert if you simply sprinkle its contents on your tongue. Meal accomplished.

While my favorite frittata is best enjoyed cold, any M.R.E. can be warmed with the "flameless heating apparatus" thoughtfully provided with each package. This uses a chemical reaction to create a hot box in which to place your food. While safely "flameless," the chemical reaction itself produces a strong odor resembling both gasoline and rotten eggs. Therefore, once your food is warm, your appetite is gone.

Another confounding aspect of the M.R.E. is the set of instructions included for the use of the heater. The wording and illustration, it seems, has not changed for years, despite the fact that it can cause complete hilarity among stressed troops, as it did today among the Brits in the truck. The sheet instructs the diner to lean the box against a "rock or something." It then includes the following illustration, complete with an object labeled "rock or something."

The real problem with M.R.E.'s, however, is the wrapping. While the heat-bonded plastic may be useful in protecting the food from nuclear fallout, it makes it impossible to actually access the food in the event you should be hungry. If you finally do manage to get the package open, you will then find each item individually wrapped in similarly impenetrable material.

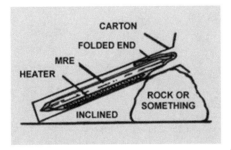

At Leatherneck, I noticed many Marines carrying their favorite enormous knives, called Ka-Bars, while walking through camp. Some Ka-Bars are nearly the size of machetes. I see them particularly among motor pool and aviation workers, and I wonder what immediate danger of hand-to-hand combat they perceive.

I have just today solved the mystery, as we struggled mightily to open the M.R.E.'s in the truck. A Ka-Bar is actually necessary to open an M.R.E. These Marines I saw, who generally work in fairly distant parts of the camp, weren't planning on violence, just lunch.

Now, I have to wonder if the design of the M.R.E. has ever damaged our hearts and minds efforts. Many generous-minded patrollers share M.R.E.'s with villages. I wonder, though, after a waving patrol is gone, how the villagers ever manage to get the food open. It's just mean to offer people lunch and then make it impossible for them to eat it. Has this ever angered a village? It would definitely anger me!

Broken truck.

CHAPTER 13

Playing I.E.D. Chicken

● DAY 96

A slim young man in unusually flowing clothes wore a strange and distant expression. He was making a swift line toward me as I stood forward of the patrol, interviewing an older gentlemen about life in his village. It was a natural place to be standing.

I was simply the person who happened to be talking to the villager, so I stood close to him. The patrol was immediately nearby, surrounding me in a semi-circle. They were my good friends, the British patrol from the broken truck, protecting me.

At first, I thought the young man might have something he urgently wanted to tell me, as villagers sometimes did. Yet something about him made us all uncomfortable. Upon seeing the man approaching from a long way off, the older gentleman I was interviewing broke off our conversation and moved hastily away. The danger was then clear.

"Lift up your shirt!" an authoritative British sergeant called to the young man while he was still a distance off but approaching at increasing speed. Translators quickly took up the yell. Other soldiers began either demonstrating the gesture or readying their rifles for him if he did not comply.

We couldn't be certain he was a suicide bomber, but all indicators seemed to blare "yes." A number of soldiers from our base were killed just this week by a bomber in our immediate area, and our nerves were stretched to breaking. Still, the patrol couldn't make a mistake and fire too early. The man continued to make his approach directly at me as the soldiers kept their best positions to fire. There wasn't time to move now.

As the person unintentionally nearest the young man, I dared not back up anyway. I held out the wild hope that by staying close to the explosion, the thick armored vest I wore might spare some of the patrol around me. If I was going to die anyway, this only made sense.

In a bizarre and incomprehensible moment, I challenged the man's now-mocking smile with my own. If I had no weapon to fight him, I would still win by keeping him from killing us all. The desperate shouting of the patrol, the readying of their raised rifles, all faded out of my hearing as the man came almost touchably nearer.

I then understood his smile. His threat was empty. He had no bomb but wouldn't mind getting himself killed as an "innocent." Sound returned. I heard the final warning of the British soldiers, trying to protect me, ready to shoot him with his next step. At the last possible moment, he lazily raised his shirt to reveal a bare chest and brushed into me as he continued on his way, through the patrol and past it.

It was a psychological game being played against us, and it was very effective. We discontinued our interviews and headed back for the base. "Go, go, go!" we yelled as we piled back into a vehicle.

I tried to move quickly, but my legs surprised me by feeling like rubber—the way they do in a nightmare when you can't outrun a monster. Both my body and mind were numb. Somehow, I was suddenly inside the jeep.

Only after we were safely returned did I allow myself to feel the appropriate, nauseating, pants-wetting fear, but the ordeal was over. The young man won only one tiny victory. I know he will often walk toward me in my dreams.

Later this evening, the gears in my mind re-engaged enough for me to wonder what that was really about—not on the level of warfare tactics but on a simply human level. Why was that young man so somehow peculiar, and what, really, would compel a young man to play with his own life and ours like he had? I had met his eyes. I had seen him closer than one would usually see a likely extremist bent on death and live to think about it after.

There was something unexpected about him—not necessarily the grim and fierce commitment of a combatant or the beatific glow of someone anticipating paradise, but almost a despondent hurt and haunted mockery of life.

● **DAY 103** Patrols are somewhat limited out of Lash right now. The last few weeks have made this the deadliest summer of British participation in the war. Nobody is saying this is the reason we are "staying in" more, but I am certain it must be.

Again, because there's not much current need for a Social Scientist here or at Leatherneck, I am being sent off back to Kandahar province. Silly poems race through my mind as I sit on another big, leaky helicopter—not one of the little Hueys that I so adore. "There was a girl who traveled far to meet her love in Kandahar . . ." It has become clear to me poetry is not my strongest suit.

It's a beautiful day, and the pilot lets us open the wide back ramp of the helicopter where its contents are loaded in. We see a huge swath of Afghanistan from high up now. The villages are tiny, but the colorful flags that fly on the walls are still clear as they blow in a rare breeze. If you lie on your belly, you can crawl right up to the edge of the ramp while still safely strapped in. I scoot up next to the gunner, and grinning outrageously, thrilled to be alive, we feel the world rush by.

Men waiting in the shade of a building.

CHAPTER 14

To Walk a Mile
for a Camel

● **DAY 105**

I don't think I'll ever be able to hear the phrase "I'd walk a mile for a Camel" in the same way again. I remember the poor hobbled camel I saw in Helmand, but here in Kandahar, I have learned that camels sometimes suffer an even worse fate after they are rendered three-footed and kept a mile out from town. The chow hall this morning was buzzing with enough uncomfortable conversation, nervous laughter, and gagging noises to get me to ask what had happened.

Apparently, a few soldiers with the duty of watching the perimeter of the camp overnight had witnessed a man approach an isolated hobbled camel. Thinking he was unobserved, he came equipped with a step-ladder, promptly sodomized the camel, and, when finished, to the hysterics of the soldiers watching from a distance, dismissed the camel with an elaborate slap on the rump—as if to celebrate the fact that he had just delivered a stellar performance. He then swaggered away, step ladder in tow.

Being the "cultural observation" person, I was asked to explain this. I can hardly imagine the research techniques that would be necessary to study bestiality formally in the context of Afghanistan, so I didn't have many answers. However, just from casual observation, I thought one might argue that it may be based generally on the unavailability or undesirability of women. Further, while at least not directed toward human beings, the practice appeared to involve an element of excessive cruelty (because of the long-term isolation and hobbling of the animal) and could be called abusive.

● **DAY 106**   Although I haven't spent as much time here as I have at other camps, Forward Operating Base Ramrod has become familiar enough to me that I anticipated the "big day" with everyone else. I just didn't realize it was today!

"Oh Great! We figured you'd get here," said the chaplain and the carpenter as they found me today and dragged me off. "We only have an hour or so to practice. You'll sing, right?"

I saw where they were leading me. It was beautiful. The chapel they had worked on for months was finished.

FOB Ramrod was more dirty and remote than Leatherneck by any imagining, but there, on the side of the camp where once the garbage was piled, was an actual wooden building, painted white. Over the months of its construction, soldiers had scrounged to find bits of clear plastic and markers. They drew and colored stained-glass patterns for the windows.

These were the soldiers of the Army's 1st Infantry Division. The young soldiers who had faced such heavy losses just earlier in the year— the friends over which the "little brother" I spoke to over warm cereal had cried. These were the soldiers who called me "Barbie."

I would sing for them. I would do anything for them.

"Perfect. Just sing the National Anthem before we start, and then I'll wink at you when you're supposed to sing Amazing Grace later. I'll say a few words, and then the newspaper people will take pictures," the chaplain instructed briskly, while nervously and proudly straightening pews and dusting off prayer books.

"Seriously? Newspaper people out here?" I asked.

"Yep. After everything that's happened to these guys, I guess the chapel's a great 'feel good' story. They're already landing!"

"Huh," I thought, as I sat down and tried to make sure I actually remembered the words to the National Anthem and Amazing Grace. Then it suddenly struck me it might be easier not to remember them at all. I felt myself choke up at their meanings in a way I never had.

I sang, and I sang every word. I just don't know how.

The service finished with smiles and hugs all around. "Hey," the Chaplain put in, "I'd like to be the one to do your wedding if I get some of that good goat you guys promise at the party! Your Marine's been telling me all about it."

"Count on it, Sir!"

● **DAY 107**   I have been studying the table arrayed with oddities and necessities, free for the taking of the troops. It tells a strange story if these are the things we might happen to need. Playing cards and holy cards, sardines and condoms, bandanas and cigarettes.

They weren't cigarettes so much as cigarillos. My favorite. I often smoked on stage in performances of Carmen (she was a tobacco worker and a gypsy, after all), and just sometimes, kept carefully hidden from my voice teacher, as I shared good scotch with good friends at favorite dark hideouts near DC.

There were moments here, though, that could only be celebrated with an excellent big cigar. The safe accomplishment of another month in theatre, for instance, which I tracked by the return of the full moon when the desert was bathed in its soft light, reflected off the sand.

Officers and contractors alike gathered together then and smoked. I was often invited among them—accepted warmly among the men if not the women, I suppose—to share a rare quiet camaraderie before uninterrupted work returned. When I think of this deployment in the future, I hope it is these moments I remember.

● **DAY 109**   I suppose that when interacting with any new culture, there are times when you are left completely taken aback if you still hold to your own perceptions of propriety or normality. It's important both to be aware of these perceptions and to hold them at bay. Today was one of those days where this became a challenge.

Translators at the Forward Operating Base deep in Kandahar province were young men from the surrounding areas, and some knew only very little English. This proved to be a problem when soldiers needed to ask or communicate something very specific to Pashto-speakers in the villages. Sometimes, the translators would simply have pleasant conversations with the villagers, completely unrelated to whatever the English-speaking soldier had hoped to say.

To help remedy this, the HTT in Kandahar province began a series of informal English lessons every evening in the translators' tent. The team was entirely men, but thinking I might have some teaching skill, they included me in the class as a new instructor. I was happy to oblige but apparently completely unprepared for the experience.

The musty tent smelled powerfully of sweat, perfume, and male presence. The center was covered with lush but stained oriental carpets, where men lounged together smoking or sharing bits of local delicacies. Instead of arranging the beds in a dormitory style, mattresses lined the walls in shadows, surrounding the central carpeted space.

I know well to keep my own cultural interpretations in check, but the place reminded me unavoidably of a bordello. Still, my academic mind admonished me that this needed to be interpreted in its own cultural context, not through a lens of my own. After all, the furniture arrangement wasn't unusual for an Afghan home.

I reprimanded myself, thinking that I must still be overly preoccupied with the camel story and had sex on the mind. How incredibly inappropriate of me! I needed to get my thinking out of the gutter, and resolved to do so.

Telling myself firmly that I had not just walked into an all-male bordello, I primly channeled a Mary Poppins personality and began with the instruction. A few men sat interestedly at my feet, and they were actually those who knew English best and hoped to come to the U.S. after the war. A few more regarded me as a fascinating curiosity.

However, from most of the rest I got the distinct impression that they found my presence repulsive. They wrinkled their nose and spat on the ground after looking at me, even though I was completely and respectfully covered. To some it had to be whispered, "Calm down. She will be gone soon." Others left the tent to wait for my exit.

Finally, toward the end of the lesson, I couldn't avoid seeing what was happening openly in front of me, so I decided to give up on Marry Poppins and address it frankly. Two men lay on one of the corner mattresses together, resting intimately intertwined. Taking a matter-of-fact approach with one of the good English speakers near me, I indicated the two and asked, "Wasn't that prohibited under the Taliban?"

"Oh, no," he responded with some shock. "The Taliban punished homosexuality. No one here is a homosexual! We just enjoy each other for pleasure." He spoke with a certain outrage that I would have confused the two.

My eyes couldn't help but dart to a fawning youth stroking the hair of an older man. Seeing this, he went on, with somewhat increasing offense. "Some of the younger ones are uneducated, but it is right that men who fight together should be very dear to each other." There was that word again, "uneducated," the same one that the Mullah had used to warn me about the men in his village.

I can't imagine feeling comfortable in that tent again. I doubt I'll give any more English lessons, but my male colleagues plan to continue teaching, as they felt liked and welcome. They still can't understand my new hesitancy to keep visiting the translators, but the clear impression I got from most the men in the tent was that I was something both offensive and disgusting for them to have to see. I have no desire to increase their offense.

I compare the experience to the occasional times circumstances have demanded that I walk through male quarters in the American tents. My presence raises a stir of attention there, but of an entirely different kind. The whistling and teasing of the American men, even when it is objectifying, is at least highly appreciative of female-ness, even at its least attractive.

I remember recently having to pass through the American men's tents, looking for someone after a patrol, as wind-blown, dusty, burnt, gaunt, and bedraggled as a person can manage to be, when a young soldier fell to his knees, exclaiming melodramatically, "My goddess of the desert! How may I serve you?" I ruffled his hair affectionately, and he comically swooned to the good-natured laughter of the tent.

Clearly, my norms of sexual interaction don't entirely apply here. I'll try to keep this in mind, both to avoid mistakes or offense in the future, and to better understand the lives of the people whose friendship and alliances we hope to gain. No matter the differences between us, if we hope to interact on a human level, we must comprehend this culture well enough to do so.

CHAPTER 15

"If You Go to a Medic, You had Better be Missing a Limb"

● **DAY 117**

I t's been a while since I have been capable of writing. In the course of this deployment, I have drunk a significant amount of tea and eaten older goat than I really care to think about. I don't mean only that the goat was old when it was slaughtered, but that it was old meat—hung out in the sun in the village square for a bit too long, so that worms were clearly visible.

At the core of my job is the need to be accepted by the communities I hope to learn about, and to do this, I can never afford to cause cultural offense. So, whenever a poor village invited me to share a sparse meal— particularly where I was allowed to observe a *shura*—I could not turn up my nose at the offerings. Whenever we might eat with a village, we made sure the patrol stopped at a bazaar on the way. That way we could arrive as good guests—providing more food than we might possibly consume.

Still, when it came down to accepting the cup of tea that preceded any real possibility of discussion—even if that tea was not quite boiled and made with the very water that was making the village sick—I would accept and drink it. Other patrol members often backed away from this offering as well as from the prepared meals, but as I was the one doing the talking, I could not excuse myself.

Like the villagers and the Marines, I fought a constant battle with intestinal bugs, but at a combat outpost past Ramrod in Kandahar, I fell truly ill. It had been drilled into me that as a female in remote combat areas, I needed to appear especially "tough" lest I embarrass my team or my program. So far, I had done well. However, I had been told, "If you go to a Medic, you had better be missing a limb."

Fortunately, the only other female on the outpost was a medic, so I shared her tent. I said nothing, but after she observed me stumbling outside the tent all night to vomit, then returning, not quite able to walk, she pressed a bag of medications into my hand. "Look," she said, "you've got to get back to a bigger base and get some help. Take the convoy leaving tomorrow morning, since it'll be the last one leaving here for a week. These medications will get you there. Then get help."

The morning was a blur to me, but I was incredibly grateful that I was in Kandahar province. This meant that I was with my fiancée's team. He was there with me the morning of the convoy, and the medic surreptitiously took him aside. I began to slip in and out of consciousness, but we made it back to a Forward Operating Base. I remember him helping me to a cot and taking off my combat boots for me. I reached out with just the strength to touch his cheek. In my confused state, I had only one thought. What a wonderful man would do something like take off my combat boots.

My world became the fabric wall of a tent. It began to seem a fascinating world, as I soon lacked the strength to turn my head and look elsewhere. With the canvas snapping gently and the sense of motion I felt, I started to believe I was sailing on a ship. The holes in the tent that let in specks of sunlight became stars over a beautiful sea. Sometimes it would occur to me that the pretty stars were merely holes, but as soon as it did, my tent would shift back to into a soothing ship. I didn't know where I was, but I believed I was going home.

It was only much later that it occurred to me that I had actually been going out of my mind. I was severely dehydrated and too weak to move, let alone acquire water by myself. I had been left alone for days in a tent lacking air conditioning in temperatures that approached 120 degrees. I was no longer vomiting because there was nothing left in my system, and it was almost three days before I could rise from my cot for any reason— nor did I have any reason.

I eventually saw that a bottle of water and box of saltines had been left for me, but they were out of my reach. At one point, I managed to fall off my cot and crawl to them. My fiancée later told me that he had checked on me, but because he usually saw that I had not touched the water, he doubted that I was dehydrated—clearly I hadn't been thirsty.

In retrospect, even if no one was willing to take me to a medic for fear of embarrassing the team or the program, someone should have at least started an IV of fluid in my arm as we were trained and equipped to do. The danger of death from heat stroke and dehydration is so great in a desert environment that we were trained to recognize the symptoms (like weakness and hallucinations) and promptly administer an IV. While the help with my boots was touching, real "caring" would have involved a desperately needed IV.

Still, I couldn't find it in my heart to be upset with my Marine who had made me a fruit salad and taken off my combat boots, although I was continuing to feel—as I had so often before—that I truly could trust no one to have my back if I was in trouble. The wedding didn't take place on this visit, but I was still sure that it would soon. I had word that huge boxes from Mom, containing my dress and veil and decorations for the party, had begun to arrive back in Helmand. I was still blissfully happy that my deepest hope was coming true.

CHAPTER 16

Really? No, Really?

● **DAY 118**

I was up and around for the first time yesterday, and today I rejoined my original team. We were to brief the incoming Marine general on the large base in Kandahar about our mission and capabilities. It went exceptionally well and received an uncharacteristically enthusiastic response from the General. There had been enough stars on collars in that room to intimidate the stoutest heart, so the fact that we left unscathed, and even with the General's approval, was a victory unimagined.

Afterward, we caught a helicopter back to Lashkar Gah. I was happy and relieved for the success, even if I was still a bit tired and weak in general. I looked forward to landing in Lash to find some dry toast and a welcoming cot. Upon our arrival, however, Lanky and Tex herded me briskly into a little room for an apparently urgent meeting.

"Next time, please don't lie when you brief a General," they said almost in unison, as if they had discussed exactly how they would address me. Horrified and confused, I asked, "What do you mean? Did I make a mistake somewhere? I am so sorry!"

"You always say that you have a Ph.D. when we present our background and qualifications. Don't do that in the future."

"Okay, I'll remove the statement if you want me to, but it is certainly not a lie. I can provide you any documentation you need to prove it. You know as well as I do that it's a job requirement for my position, and that it would have been vetted."

Fortified against invaders and the wind.

"Fine, then it's true, but that doesn't matter. It still comes off as a lie, and we don't want the General perceiving us as liars."

"Why on earth would it come off as a lie?"

"Because you are too young, and you're female, and you're clearly Hispanic or somehow otherwise 'ethnic.' In our society nobody in their right mind would believe that you have a Ph.D., let alone from Notre Dame."

My heart sank when I realized that this was about the odd combination of my age, gender, and background, and I was dismayed why Tex, a Hispanic woman, was nodding in agreement! After being surrounded by the extreme example of gender prejudice that enveloped us in Afghanistan, I had thought that we as Americans would have become less prone to it. Still, I responded:

"We were *instructed* to brief our career and educational background, and that brief was approved before we left training. I do not dwell on my background, but I want the General to know that he has a qualified team doing this work. How is it any different from you listing your own qualifications, which add to the capability of the team just like mine do?"

"The difference is that a General could believe me, a respectably older white male, but he could not believe you. It may not be fair, but it's true. I come off as credible."

I wondered if this was true. The General, in fact, and generals I had briefed before him in my career, seemed to have no problem taking me seriously or finding me credible. The problem, it appeared, was only with my team itself.

Lanky's words perhaps revealed more about what he himself believed than what might have been true of the General. He was talking about his own cultural attitude, and it was one in which the idea of an educated young minority female seemed incomprehensible. Frustrated, I went on.

"Would it be preferable, then, that I introduce myself to the General as an incompetent and arbitrarily selected wench off the street who brings no abilities or qualifications to the table other than my sheer willingness to risk my neck?"

"That would be far more believable."

The saddest part about this conversation to me was not the prejudice, with which I was already intimately familiar, but the sudden realization that Lanky and Tex, my own team, didn't feel the same way about me as I felt about them. I actually thought the world of them. They could not have thought well of me and simultaneously accused me of lying.

Having been formed by the lessons of my first team in Iraq, I automatically considered my teammates to be my brothers and sisters, and I treated them as such. I assumed the same was true for them. Now, in the light of their hard glares, I could see past my happy optimism for the first time to the cold fact that they simply couldn't stand me.

At times we faced the unknowable threats of the villages together, and thinking them my closest comrades, I was committed and comfortable with the idea of protecting them with my life. Clearly, the feeling wasn't mutual. Again, I realized that whatever I faced, I faced alone.

"Would you prefer I did not serve on this team?" I asked.

"You know how we feel. Whether you stay or go is your decision. However, I would support you strongly in a decision to go."

Slow though I am, I got the distinct impression that I was not particularly welcome. With Lanky's "support," I submitted a request to the head of the program that I be transferred to another team. The leader of the Kandahar team put in an immediate request that I be transferred to them, as he thought my work for their team had been excellent. Now all I can do is wait, hope, and in the meantime, keep doing my work shoulder-to-shoulder with my teammates with what dignity I can, despite the fact that I feel like a fool.

DAY 121 The requests for transfer were swiftly denied. My heart is heavy, as I still have a long while left to my deployment, and I can no longer enjoy the useful illusion that I work among friends. Perhaps it's just my upset over the transfer issue that has me anxious, but I worry that I have not heard from my fiancée in three days.

I suppose this is reasonable, as phones and email communications go down regularly, and he could have gone on a mission somewhere inaccessible. Three days, however, is unusual. We write every day, and often he writes me a few times in a day.

He bought me a cell phone that works in-country just so he could call me. I think he gets a bit jealous and likes the ability to know where I am. I don't mind it. I want to reassure him. That's what makes it unusual that he hasn't called or written, and that I can't reach him.

If he were planning on a long mission, he would normally mention this to me. I would send him some thoughts to keep him company along the way. Communications go out, but technical issues are quickly fixed.

Sometimes communications black out when someone on the base is killed, but this lasts only as long as it takes to notify the family. It's usually one or two days at the maximum. I supposed a number of these circumstances could have piled up at once, but still, three days is just a tiny bit over the line of "odd."

I can't let my mind run wild thinking the phones are out because he might have been killed. That's a wild assumption. I know better.

I am obsessing. Nothing is wrong. I am sure.

DAY 122 No word. Has anyone heard about anything going on in Kandahar? Surely we would know about casualties by now. Wouldn't we?

● **DAY 123**   No word. I cannot find any logical explanation for this much time passing that does not involve something tragic. No one is talking about deaths, and I think the program would have somehow gotten the word out if we lost a member. However, if he or someone on the Kandahar team was wounded, perhaps that word wouldn't get out as quickly.

● **DAY 124**   No word. If he is wounded, is he alone at a medical facility somewhere? Would anyone know to contact me? What if nobody at the hospital understands that I'm really his wife—that only a matter of weeks separates me from that fact. Until then, though, how would they know to call me? What do I do?

● **DAY 125**   No word. I have no logic left in me. Please, somebody just tell me he is alive.

● **DAY 126**   He emailed. He's alive. He's unhurt. There was no tragedy. That's enough for me.

The message I got from him was brief. It was to tell me that his house had gone into foreclosure. It was unbelievably better news than hearing his patrol had been attacked!

"That's okay, my love!" I wrote back with immense relief. "I have a house where we can live, and it's silly to have two. You know, though, foreclosing on a house can affect your security clearance, and once we are married, it will affect mine too. How much do you owe? We're a team, and maybe I might have enough money to prevent the foreclosure. Don't worry about a thing. I'll find a way to help."

I called Mom, and even she is willing to lend me money to prevent my future husband from foreclosing. We just need some sense of how much is owed. I wrote to ask him, reassuring him that we would help.

● **DAY 129**   No word again for the last three days. When I finally sent him a desperate email today, he did respond. "If you think you or your family has any right to ask me about money, you've got the wrong idea about our relationship. You need to realize this before we get married. I don't have to tell you a thing about my personal affairs."

His message went on. How dare I email him and expect a response? Didn't I understand the stress he was under? "Every time I pass a doorway on a patrol, I don't know if someone inside is planning to kill me!" he complained.

If I wasn't crying, I would have almost had to laugh. Of course I understood that kind of stress—it was precisely the same stress I encountered on every patrol. However, he faced that danger as a big well-armed male, while my five-foot self was still without the paperwork to carry a gun. I was vividly reminded of our first patrol when I was nabbed into one of those frightening doorways he mentioned while he stood by.

He was right. I did need to realize all of this before we got married. I was willing to risk everything for him—not only my life, but the money that my Mom and I had worked so desperately to earn. Again, the feeling didn't appear to be mutual.

I believed his "I don't need to tell you a thing," was meant to extend into other aspects of our relationship as well. It reminded me of the angry words of abusive men I had known before. With my heart breaking, I realized I would not be marrying this man.

Because the HTT community is small, ugly rumors are already starting to reach me. They may be true or they may be simply intended to hurt me further. It's being whispered that the reason my Marine didn't want me to know much about his house was because another woman, who he kept at home while he trained and deployed with me, was living there.

If this was so well-known, why hadn't someone told me sooner? Apparently, this wasn't the least bit uncommon among men who deploy frequently. Was I the "other woman," or was she? My world and hopes were shattered, and I was utterly alone—without even a friend in whom I could confide.

I wandered out into the desert night and wept at the full moon. *Inshallah*. I never understood God's will, but I trusted it. Still, I ached. The thing I believed I wanted most—a good marriage to a strong man and happy children—was not to be mine. As important as it seemed, perhaps this isn't what I was meant for after all.

I now wonder if what I truly wanted was to believe in a hero. I came to idolize my fiancée because I believed him heroic—a fearless defender of good in a troubled world—strong where I knew myself to be weak, brave where I knew myself to be afraid. Even when he showed me otherwise, I refused to see. I have decided to open my eyes now, and what I do see is beautiful.

The heroism I so longed to believe in is all around. Everyone here might be flawed and frightened like me. The amazing thing is that they are nevertheless risking everything to make an effort toward a safer, better world for others, as best as they can see how. I don't need to look for heroism, I just need to see it.

● DAY 130 I've been too preoccupied over the last several days to write much about work, but much has transpired. In stark contrast to my distraught mood, our British colleagues cheerfully put in a most unexpected research request. They were my two closest friends at Lashkar Gah, "Action Man" and "Slasher."

Slasher, my usual British counterpart on patrols (about whom it was rumored that I shared the dubious honor of once having gone to war instead of jail), had an incredible talent for respecting and commanding respect from Afghan village leaders, and he was always insightful in his analysis of them. He was also about as strong and stout as anyone could wish to stand beside in a fight, and I was proud to call him a friend.

Action Man was distinguished and gracious. At this point in his career, he was more prone to sit and give thoughtful consideration to the means of touching hearts and minds with a message of peace and understanding than he was to engage in any action. However, a toy called Action Man was the U.K. equivalent of America's G.I. Joe, and like G.I. Joe, our soldier tended to wear every conceivable gadget attached to his vest of armor—as if he was prepared to go into the field for months.

"Could you please explain what's funny around here?" they asked.

"Just about everything," I answered, raising an aching and exhausted head off my desk. They guffawed. It took me a moment to realize they were actually asking for a definition of local humor.

In truth, it was a brilliant question. There so was much to it. The troops had noticed that they possessed no shared sense of humor with the Afghan men they engaged.

The Afghans would tell a story, laugh hysterically, and the Brits, because of some apparent meanness or mockery or even downright grossness in the jibe, wouldn't be sure whether to laugh at all. They just didn't "get" what was funny, but they didn't want to fail to fit in and interact in friendly ways. No one likes a stick-in-the-mud, Afghan villagers included.

There was also an even more interesting application to the question. What if we wanted to "make fun" of someone? What if we wanted to paint extremists or Taliban supporters in a clownish light to the villages?

What would make them seem ridiculous to local people, rather than frightening and powerful? What if someone could draw a really funny cartoon? Make up a slogan that stuck? If we didn't understand the local humor such attempts would surely fall flat, or even backfire.

The question of what constitutes humor—what it is that makes us laugh when it does—is one of those issues philosophers and psychologists have debated for eons. I hoped to avoid that mire entirely and aim for a practical solution. Certainly there were specific and identifiable cultural differences in humor. Being around the Brits demonstrated that! So it seemed right to approach the question from that angle.

The next problem, then, was how to ask the question that allows someone to articulate what they think is funny. "Could you please explain the nature of humor in your cultural context?" while it was the actual question we wanted answered, would never work.

Instead, it would be necessary to interview as many people as possible with as revealing but simple questions as we could develop, and then compile and analyze those answers. The questions I proposed were:

- What's the funniest story you've ever heard?
- What makes you laugh when you think of it?
- Tell me a good joke!

No matter how clever I thought those questions were, however, there was no way to know if they would really make any sense to nearby residents unless we somehow "tested" them on local people first. The translators were a perfect solution. They could both understand the questions and tell us, in English, if and why they made sense or not.

There was a South African contractor working for the Brits. He was the nicest gentleman, and always talked about his gorgeous wife and their pack of giant mastiffs at home on his ranch. I often asked to see pictures of his four-foot-tall "puppies," as we both called them, and he always had new ones to show.

His job, whatever else it might have included, involved having tea every day with the translators, both to gain some language skills and to offer them a constant sort of interface with the military, so things would be friendly in their camp. We asked if we could accompany him.

"Sure," he said, "I'd be very glad of the company—especially the women."

"That's nice," I responded, a bit flattered, "but why?"

"Because there's this guy over there . . . and he's gay . . . ," he said quietly, looking sideways.

I was suddenly irate with him for his apparent homophobia and simple prejudice. "What on *earth* would that have to do with anything? Do you think he's suddenly not someone to have tea with, then? Do you think that makes him a bad translator? A bad person? What exactly is your problem?!"

I ranted furiously. I had always been a bit sensitive to the subject since I became so proud of my Dad's honesty in coming out. I wasn't going to let this guy get away with something like what he had implied.

"No, no!" he said, waiving his hands innocently. "It's nothing like that! It's just that since I've been going over, he's said he likes me, and I didn't really know how to react at first, and now the more I go, the more he thinks I like him too, and I don't know what to do to fix the impression without being incredibly rude—which is just the opposite of what I want. I was just hoping you being there might make things less, um, uncomfortable. Maybe you'd seem like—how do the Americans say it—a 'beard'!"

Understanding his issue, then, I tagged along, clipboard in hand. The translators were amused by the whole line of questioning. They understood and approved of the survey—though they and my team made modifications to the questions—and they answered with some funny stories of their own. Mostly, though, their happy conversation centered not on humor but on who liked who in the tent!

Now it became clear that the translator who concerned the soldier wasn't the only man who seemed to like other men. I thought immediately, of course, of the translators' tent in Kandahar, where sex was happening openly. Here I found myself again!

Confused, it occurred to me that perhaps I was thinking of homosexuality in strictly American cultural terms, where I tend to consider it a fairly rare personal trait. Something else entirely seemed to be happening here. It would be too unimaginably enormous a statistical anomaly for *two* whole translator's camps of men to, by happenstance, all possess a single rare trait.

Something unnatural, mathematically, at least, was going on here, if I continued to think of homosexuality in its Western sense. Okay, I thought, I don't get it, but I guess I get that I don't get it. It was the same sort of thought that had occurred to me so often in this deployment—the thought that emphasized my utter foreignness, and also the potential usefulness of my lens as such a complete outsider—since, perhaps, I first saw a goat in a tree.

Completely aside from the sex issue, we have since spent the last several days executing our research plan. It is perhaps the strangest one I've attempted so far. We drive to a village perimeter in a convoy of armored vehicles, pile out dramatically camouflaged and geared-up like Rambo, enter into the village in a patrol formation, and ask, essentially, "So, heard any good jokes lately?"

Sadly, there was one joke I heard over and over, from almost every one of my interviewees. I had heard it before, quite frequently from men I interviewed prior to initiating our research on humor. It was so common I supposed it was the local equivalent of "Why did the chicken cross the road?"

When it was first told to me, I wondered if it was some odd way of telling me that women weren't worth much. It always went something like this:

"My father is dead and everyone has sex with my mother. I found out that my neighbor slept with her. Then his cousin. Then his cousin's brother. I realized a simple solution to the problem. I killed my mother." (This is always followed by gales of hilarity. It is no wonder that our forces are often confused where humor lies, or when to laugh.)

Anyway, I hope I've discovered a bit more depth to the local humor than that, and I hope I've also sorted out some of the context in which the joke is funny. I guess it's truly been a good thing that I've been so occupied while my life has been going so poorly otherwise. I'd rather be here tonight, just having finished the report, than alone in my bunk, or wandering the camp, thinking about anything else. I'm including my report below.

Human Terrain Team (HTT) AF-6
Research Results Update

Background

HTT-6 has been tasked with investigating the Afghan, particularly Pashtu, sense of humor in support of ██████████████ efforts to integrate culturally-applicable comedic campaigns intended to discredit Taliban personalities. This is a difficult question that warrants special attention, as humor is notoriously difficult to define in any culture, and an error could result in a loss of ISAF credibility.

HTT has taken the following three approaches:

1) Engaging willing Afghans with these questions:
   - Can you give an example of something that makes you laugh?
   - What makes something funny?
   - What is the funniest joke you know or story you've heard?
2) Extending an inquiry to the HTT Research Reachback Center (RRC) on both the methodology of assessing a culturally unique brand of humor and on any previous work available on defining Afghan humor.
3) Conducting open-source research on humor or comedy presented by Afghans and on reporting of such humor from non-Afghan sources.

Summary

HTT has begun approach 1 by vetting the proposed interview questions with interpreters present on LKG. The interpreters have confirmed the intelligibility and applicability of the questions, and, as targets of opportunity, have also provided responses.

HTT has found certain themes in these initial responses to be highly consistent with open source research and previous engagements with Afghans where humor was present but not the focus of inquiry.

HTT confirms that precedent exists, both historically and psychologically, to indicate that humorous degradation of the Taliban, if culturally appropriate, may strike an important resonance, even if villagers remain fearful to make such jokes themselves.

KEY FINDINGS

- The portrayal of a personality as a Hashish addict will most likely be regarded by Pashtuns as both appropriately humorous and discrediting.
- The misapplication of logic is a key element of traditional Afghan humor, highly applicable to Pashtuns. The portrayal of a personality as educated or pompous but illogical will successfully and humorously discredit an individual.
- "Mullah Nasurdin" is a humorous fictional figure highly popular in Afghanistan as in the rest of the Islamic world. Well-researched references will be accepted and appreciated.

RESEARCH RESULTS

The Afghan, and particularly Pashtu, tradition of humor is oral (rather than written or pictorial) and is integrally dependent on the spoken language and its intonation. Nevertheless, a written or pictorial message may communicate this oral humor if it follows upon a theme already established in the oral tradition.

Several themes were repeatedly confirmed:
- Addicts, especially those with a dependency on Hashish, were consistently the butt of jokes.
  - Beginning a story by stating that it involved an addict almost immediately produced laughter among Pashtuns interviewed, prior to the delivery of any humorous outcome.
  - Occasionally, when conducting interviews in other contexts, HTT has heard persons disliked by the interviewees laughingly referred to as "Hashish addicts." It was at times unclear if the persons were in fact addicted or if this was a humorous disparaging accusation. Most likely, both were true.
  - The portrayal of a personality as a Hashish addict will most likely be regarded by Pashtuns as both appropriately humorous and discrediting.
- The misapplication of logic is the most consistent recurring theme in Pashtu and Afghan humor investigated thus far.
  - Traditional jokes featuring the personality of Mullah Nasurdin exemplify this brand of humor, although it occurs in other contexts as well.

- In the paper "Intentional and Unintentional Afghan Humor: 'Local Logic' at its Best,"* Don and Alleen Nilsen state: "To Afghans, the stories are very humorous, but to Westerners, the stories are illogical and enigmatic. Mullah Nasrudin stories are perfect examples of local logic, and in fact, they are ways of testing even this local logic."
- Examples of this humor follow:
  - "Mullah Nasrudin said that he was as strong now as he had been as a youth. When asked for proof, he said, 'When I was a youth, there was a huge boulder that I was not able to lift. I am still not able to lift that same boulder, so you can see that I am as strong now as I was then.' "†
  - "How old are you, Mullah?" someone asked. 'Three years older than my brother,' he replied. 'How do you know that?' 'Reasoning. Last year, I heard my brother tell someone that I was two years older than him. A year has passed. That means that I am older by one year. I shall soon be old enough to be his grandfather."‡
- Perhaps the most discrediting and humorous aspect of the Hashish addict, addressed above, is his loss of logic. This is seen in the following example, which is not self-evidently humorous to a western listener.
  - "Two Hashish addicts were smoking by a river. One decided to take off his clothes and cross the river, but was swept away. He waved to his friend for help, but his friend only waved back responding, 'don't worry, brother, now that you are part of the river, I will see you everywhere.' "
- Portraying a personality as guilty of faulty reasoning, especially if that person presents themselves to be educated, like the Mullah, may be perceived as humorous and derogatory.
  - Mullah Nasrudin hardly knew what to preach on a Friday. He began by asking the congregation, "Who knows what I'm going to say?" Nobody raised their hands. He said, "I will not preach to stupid people," and left. Next Friday, he asked the

---

* Available through the ERIC database at http://www.eric.ed.gov/
† op cit
‡ Archive available at http://www.afghan-web.com/culture/jokes.html

same question. Everybody raised their hands. He said, "Good then. Why should I preach?" The following Friday, the people wanted a sermon and had a new strategy. Half raised their hands and half did not. The Mullah said "Good. The half that know, tell the half that don't."*

- Other established themes of oral tradition were evidenced but were less suited to ISAF purposes. These included flatulence,† vulgar language, and violence toward women.
  - Sadly, the most repeated joke in interviews was a series of variations on this:
    - A man's mother had been known to sleep with all the men of the village. Upon realizing this, the man killed his mother, because it was more efficient than having to kill so many men.
    - Even this, however, can be categorized as a play on logic.

PRECEDENCE

There is yet no evident local humor regarding the Taliban in the TF Helmand. This is likely due to the seriousness of the Taliban's imminent threat in the daily lives of villagers. Nevertheless, precedence exists, both psychologically and historically, to indicate that such humor, if culturally appropriate, may strike an important resonance—even if villagers are afraid of being "caught in the act" of making such jokes themselves.

- In *Cultures of the Comic under Socialism,* Justine Gill states that Afghans turned to humor as a safe release mechanism for their discontent under Russian occupation. She writes:

In the Afghan milieu, these types of safety-valve tales which attack certain institutions by using individuals as butts of jokes and are often filled with double entendre are common traditionally. This tradition is partially seen in the Afghan heritage of "Mullah Nasruddin" jokes, common throughout the Islamic world. Mullah Nasruddin was a character through whom criticism and analysis

---

* Archive available at http://www.virtualafghan.com/fun
† In addition to HTT interviews, see "Searching for Comedy in the Muslim World: Reflections of a Harvard Joke Collector" at http://www.wrmea.com/archives/Jan_Feb_2009/0901035.html

of people in power, religion, common sayings, 'folk knowledge' and paradoxes could be presented.*

- In *Jokes and Their Relation to the Unconscious*, one of the principal works dealing with the attempt to define humor in any culture, Freud argues:

  Where a joke is not an aim in itself . . . there are only two purposes that it may serve . . . It is either a hostile joke (serving the purpose of aggressiveness, satire, or defense) or an obscene joke (serving the purpose of exposure).

- The mechanism of humor may allow for an essential release of tensions that are disallowed expression in daily village life, and may therefore solidify an affinity with ISAF in a way that could not otherwise be achieved.

---

* Paper available at http://slavic.princeton.edu/download/files/Justine%20Gill.pdf

Everyday life.

CHAPTER **17**

Incoming!

● DAY 131

Over my dinner break, I received an emailed invitation to a release party for the Kanye West CD I sang on between deployments. I would not be there, but I felt embraced by my first love—my music. I still couldn't bring myself to eat, so I walked to the most remote area of the base I could find, next to a perimeter wall, where I could be alone and bother no one with my voice.

Like on the first day of this deployment, I found myself preoccupied with a song. The music always arrives in my head before I realize how it is meaningful to my situation. In my mind, I heard over and over Kathleen Ferrier singing the simple, haunting old melody that begins *Che Faro?*

What is life, if life is without you?
Who am I, if I am not your love?
Where am I to go? What am I to do?
What will be my life if now my life is not with you?

Ferrier was a Contralto whose voice somehow captured the world's own feelings during World War I. When she died unexpectedly young, she received a funeral grander than the Queen of England's. To me now, it is finally easy to understand why the few songs she was famous for spoke to everyone who had lost so much to a war. One way or another, war seems to rob us of what it is that we love and leaves us wondering who, exactly, we are in its wake.

I sang. I poured my heart and my hurt into the aria, and it was let free. As I reached the final highest notes, I calmly registered that I was hearing a descending whistle over the melody, almost as if it were accompanying me.

I was utterly without sleep and my mind wasn't very sharp. As it quickly grew louder and I finally registered its meaning, the aria ended in a shout of "INCOMING!!!" for anyone close enough to hear me yell. As Lashkar Gah was rarely attacked, no early-warning siren had sounded. The rocket sailed over my head and impacted on just the opposite side of the wall next to which I stood.

I had a decision to make. The wall provided some cover, but was useless if the next rocket should land on my side. There was good hard cover further inside the base, but I would have to cross a wide open area with no cover to get there. I counted to ten. No second rocket had fallen. Maybe no more rockets would come.

I broke to run for better cover, and as soon as I was away from the protection of the wall, other rockets began sailing by. Now I heard the theme to *Chariots of Fire* in my mind as I ran, and I did one thing that I thought my Mediterranean assets were never equipped to do. I moved like a gazelle.

I slid into a building and out of sheer exhaustion, heartbreak, and relief, laughed and laughed at the ridiculousness of the whole circumstance in which I found myself. A number of similarly relieved British soldiers joined me, making bawdy jokes about where they had been when the rockets hit. We all laughed until our eyes watered.

● **DAY 132**   At Lash, there are a variety of government employees. There are the British troops, there are U.S. State Department employees, and there are USAID workers. Everyone gets along nicely, generally, or they rarely intersect.

Today was one of those days when a bit of cultural translation—not regarding the Afghan communities, but just us here at the base—was in order. Charging through the hall approached a young USAID worker, his blonde hair in a floppy style, which he had to flick constantly out of his eyes. ("Why not cut it?," I couldn't help but wonder, as did everyone else, but I never asked.)

"Guys!" he announced as he passed our office, "I just made the scariest, coolest, most awesome mistake ever!"

Not able to resist that introduction, I took the bait. Tex scowled at me for doing so. "Okay, what happened?"

"I met this little British guy with the most unbelievable knife. You should have seen it. It was fancy and wicked."

"Oh, you met a Gurkha. Yeah, those guys are amazing, and their knives are works of art." The Gurkhas are the elite of the fighting culture of Nepal, and they have served with British forces for well over a hundred years. The famous quote about them goes, "If a man says he's not afraid of death, he's either lying or he's a Gurkha."

"I didn't know who he was—I just asked him for a knife." I swallowed hard at that. I knew something about Gurkhas' knives.

They were prized emblems of their service, and they were also fiercely, almost legendarily effective. Ornate with an elegantly curved blade, they were also beautiful. I knew every service had a knife they thought symbolic and particularly loved. I thought of the Marines and their Ka-Bars.

The young man, struggling to open a cardboard shipping container, asked the first person to pass him, "Hey, got a knife?" That's perhaps the most interesting thing you could ask a Gurkha, and also, perhaps, the most inappropriate.

The Gurkha officer smiled amusedly. "Sure, my friend. Want to see something?" he asked.

In the storeroom, there was a stack of perhaps 40 cardboard boxes, flattened and tightly bound to save space. Before the young man could nod, the Gurkha drew his knife and sliced through them, top to bottom, as if he were slicing the air. Then, delicately but expertly, with just the tip of his blade, he cut our floppy-haired friend's box so that it fell open at his feet

To the utter shock of the already-stunned young man, the Gurkha then winked, drew the blade across his own hand, wiped the blood from the knife, and sheathed it back at his waist.

"Why'd you do that?" our friend managed to ask.

The elegant officer answered, "When this knife is drawn, it's drawn to spill blood, son. It doesn't go into a sheath until it has."

The Gurkha walked away whistling, and the young man, here in a war

Slasher alongside.

and yet so rarely aware of the actual business of fighting, joked he felt the sudden need to change his pants. I guess we can all continually benefit from understanding our neighbors a little better.

● **DAY 133**   Thank goodness I've been spending so much time seeing what transpires in the Afghan gentlemen's tents lately. I think it helped me answer a question today. It regarded the same difficult issue that faced the South African contractor. I wasn't sure how to react the first time, but now I hope I'm understanding a bit better. Though my response was by necessity tentative, I can only hope that it was helpful.

A soldier took me aside to visit in an unfrequented alley between tents. Though he wasn't a member of a Special Operations unit, I knew him to work closely with one. The secrecy with which he approached me made me think his question must have to do with something that would interest James Bond—something shadowy and classified.

The Special Operations community, like HTT in a certain sense, frequently has the responsibility of building close relationships with village communities. The soldier was comfortably familiar with the local practice of men wrapping languid arms around one another's shoulders, embracing fondly, etc., and he had been trained to understand these behaviors as "just the way guys got along here."

However, he was bothered by a conversation he had just had with one of his local contacts, and sought me out afterward. The slightly older gentleman took him aside to tell him that "he was not like the others, who simply sleep with each other." (This in itself was news to the understandably unprepared soldier.)

The older man wanted him to know that he had genuine affection for the soldier, and would not "use him thus." He wanted to reassure the soldier that he actually enjoyed and preferred to sleep with men, much as the Mullah had tried to reassure me regarding his preference.

The soldier, maintaining his friendship with the local man, thought he could put an end to the matter by telling the man he had a wife and children back home. He even pulled out a family photo from his uniform pocket. "I do too," said the older man with confusion, as if this was no obstacle.

The soldier then replied, with as much diplomacy as he could, that while he was flattered, he did not enjoy being with men. "Ah, my sweet friend, but you keep your face so beautifully smooth," said the older man, running a finger down his regulation-shaved cheek.

My best advice to the bewildered soldier was to grow his beard from that day, as most Special Operations personnel are free to do. I am just learning there seems to be significance to beardlessness in Pashtun culture. However, American military grooming regulations are extremely strict.

If that soldier is not actually attached to a Special Operations unit, I don't know if he will be allowed to grow a beard. I wonder how much of a problem this might be for other American men, or if they are even aware that the problem might exist. I wonder if this particular bit of cultural confusion could be widespread, or if I am witnessing something more isolated.

It's funny, the South African contractor mentioned needing a "beard," to keep him from seeming available to the Pashtun man, but I doubt he knew how literally it might have been true!

Female Engagement Team

CHAPTER 18

The First U.S.M.C. Female Engagement Team

● DAY 135

B ack to Leatherneck again. I have been fine most days, but I don't know how I got through last night. While we were at Lash, the beautiful wedding dress arrived here from my Mom. It has been stored on my bunk because there is nowhere else to put it. Now I must sleep curled up next to it. I'm afraid this requires more strength than I actually possess.

I am throwing myself into the commander's new project, which I find fascinating. He has slotted HTT to develop and train teams of female Marines to operate in Afghan communities, much as I do. As confused as my feelings are about women on the front lines (or in the case of a counterinsurgency, outside the wire), I see an undisputable logic to the teams.

In a region as completely gender-segregated as southern Afghanistan, it would either be necessary for women to function outside the wire or for the Marines to deal only with one half of the population, which would be a strategic detriment to their efforts. Our war here is not one of bullets and bombs, no matter how much they fly. Our victory can only be found in the people themselves, and therefore women, as true and full warriors, have become necessary in order to reach the country's women.

The most significant individual act of warfare in Afghanistan is not in causing harm or damage, though one must be highly skilled and continually prepared to do so in defense of innocent life, but in creating true human connection. The women I first spoke with, so compelled to "outpace" their brothers in all the demands of being a Marine, I dare argue have some natural advantage to this task, in the same way that men have other natural advantages.

If the people of Afghanistan sincerely support the Taliban, al Qa'ida and other extremist terror groups, then no matter how many terrorists the U.S. might fight and kill, endless replacements will crop up in their place and the war will continue indefinitely. However, if the people realize that they no longer wish to live under the oppression of extremist violence, rally to create their own future, and cooperate with Western forces to help identify and eliminate the terrorist "hold-outs" that threaten us along with them, then the war is truly won, and Afghanistan is its own.

Realizing the impossibility of winning a war for the hearts and minds of an entire country if only attempting to engage men, the commander has ordered the official creation of the United States Marine Corps Female Engagement Team (USMC FET)—the first team of its kind. While there had been a "Lioness" program in Iraq, where female Marines were used to screen Iraqi women for explosives in order to ensure safety but avoid cultural faux pas, the members of the FET would be trained to actually speak to, assist, and otherwise engage with Afghan women outside the wire—in the homes and communities where the women lived (and were typically not allowed to leave).

Because HTT is already doing precisely this work in addition to our other responsibilities, it falls to us to train, mentor, and serve on the first iteration of the team.

● **DAY 137** We stood at perfectly still attention as roll call was read. Each name was answered with "Here!" until the roll reached Cahir. No answer. "Sgt. Cahir?" No answer.

Finally, louder, " Sgt. Cahir?" Someone finally answered for him.

"Sgt. Bill Cahir, United States Marine Corps, Killed in Action, August 13th, 2009."

Complete silence followed.

Before us was a pair of boots and a standing rifle hung with a set of dog tags. Grown men, strong men, cried as they passed them, touching the tags with a final goodbye. The Marine had lived an exceptional life.

Sgt. Cahir was an example of the unique breed of person who chooses to serve in the American military today. He was a Penn State graduate. He had a renowned career as a journalist. He was a national political figure—both a 2008 candidate for Congress from Pennsylvania and a Congressional committee staffer for Senator Ted Kennedy.

Following September 11th, he was already too old for military accession. A man of his age should never have survived boot camp. He worked and pleaded for an exception to the rule. He was allowed to go to boot camp, and he came out a Marine.

He chose to become an enlisted man—a "grunt" as we said with all affection—and he loved his role as an "Old Sergeant" to young Marines. He had every qualification to become an officer, but he wanted to do his work as close to the ground, and as close to the people of Iraq and Afghanistan, as possible. He was assigned to Civil Affairs—a job we all called the Peace Corps with rifles on steroids.

His work was that of heroes—the truest warriors of a counterinsurgency. He sought to fulfill the needs of Afghan communities by building strong relationships with them. More importantly, he sought to give them the protection and the knowledge to fulfill their needs themselves. He was entirely about serving people, both his Marines and the people of the countries he visited.

He was killed by a single sniper's bullet as he returned from one of the villages he loved to help. The poor man was always frustrated trying to explain that his name was not pronounced "Ca-here" but instead like "Care." It seemed to define him. Care he did.

After the evening service, a hand touched my shoulder in the quiet. An officer brushed aside a real tear. "Your guitar. Do you think you could get your guitar?" he asked.

I retrieved it from a tent and ran to catch up with him. I wasn't sure what he wanted me to do, but I wasn't going to say no to anything the Marines needed at this point. I've been to as many funerals as anyone, I suppose, but I never felt the intensity of collective emotion that was present here.

He led me to a boarded facility that some very senior leaders used for an office. They sat, and brought what food they could find. "Play something, the way you do. We just don't want to be in the quiet tonight. Play something beautiful."

I played to put an end to their sadness. Somehow, though, it became a part of my own. I hope the "caring" the sergeant did so well triumphs for all of us in the end.

● **DAY 139** I find myself looking out across an impromptu plywood classroom of young Marines—pretty bright faces, some shadowed with worry, and each wearing a flawless bun and the fierce determination that makes a Marine a Marine.

They have been plucked from their jobs all around Afghanistan to attend the selection and training for the FET, simply based upon the fact that they are women. They are officers with advanced degrees and enlisted girls who looked to me as though they have been teleported from their high schools. Their occupational specialties and training range from aircraft mechanics to food service workers to intelligence personnel.

While each had obviously joined one of the most adventurous branches of the military and were deployed to Afghanistan, many are extremely wary of the idea of venturing outside the wire. It is not unusual for military personnel to spend entire deployments without ever leaving the base to which they are assigned. My first job, both formally and informally, was to try to give the ladies a realistic perception of what the experience is like.

Especially for the youngest learners, it is hard to express the lesson that the people of the villages, who sometimes may seem exotic and sometimes may seem frightening, are simply people—possessing the same needs and issues that we all share and equally deserving of respect and consideration—when I have to mitigate that statement with the warning that some of the people may occasionally try to kill you. And they won't be wearing a uniform to help you differentiate them from the innocent people you will be trying to help.

Sergeant Cahir's story wasn't far from anyone's mind. I found it both beautiful and poignant, especially because of this, that every single one of the Marine women embraced this dangerous dichotomy, and not one backed down from the commitment to help her Afghan sisters. I had to wonder how many of them also knew about Paula. I had to wonder what I was encouraging them, by training them, to do.

My job, nevertheless, was to boil down ethnographic technique into what I officially titled a "field-expedient model for conflict environments." Academia aside, I needed to teach the girls what to look for in order to quickly assess a village or home. They needed to know how to spot danger and how to spot need. They needed to know how to pick up on social cues and learn how to avoid offense in entirely foreign environments.

I realize now that I need to teach analytical thinking skills that seem natural to some and entirely revelatory to others. I need to make everything both practical and immediately useful. I will work on tomorrow's lesson plan tonight.

Oh, and back to my pet peeve—the chow hall was supposed to open yesterday, and it didn't. We all got excited for nothing. I have recently learned from knowledgeable sources that it will not open for some time yet.

It was built to use American electricity! Of course, there is no available electricity in that voltage here. The kitchen will have to be ripped out and re-fitted. Morale has taken a nose-dive, my own included.

● **DAY 140** It's the final day of training for those who have made the selection. With my teammates I have taken to acting out possible village scenarios for the FET selectees and letting them practice their new skills. (They like it best when I play the grouchy old grandma—complete with my ragged black shawl.) I am *proud* of these Marines. I am also proud that I will serve with them, continuing my HTT work but also co-assigned to be a guiding member of the FET on their early missions.

The ladies had other instructors to refresh their firearms and tactical training. As a new member of the FET, I asked that I too might have the firearms paperwork issue cleared up, and shot a particularly excellent qualification on the developing range to prove my accuracy. Still the range wasn't certified, so it didn't count. The ladies had officially qualified before they came overseas.

I found it funny, however, that the Commander at Leatherneck, in a caring and fatherly way, vehemently insisted today that no female Marine would be allowed to patrol without a rifle because it would be too great a danger. He announced this in my presence without noticing the irony or making any attempt to see to my safety as well. Of course, as a Govie,

I wasn't his responsibility in the way that the Marines were. Still, a little humanity would have been very appreciated.

An odd thought occurred to me. I had never actually spoken to the Commander. I perhaps wasn't even an actual person in his eyes. As the team leader, it was Lanky's job to coordinate our work within the command structure, and information could only be "passed up the chain," or back down to us, through him. Tex and I had never had so much of a conversation as "hello" except by Lanky's proxy.

Was the Commander even consciously aware of my firearms issue? Was that why he spoke the way he did? Was he aware that the work he read was mine? Who knew what he actually knew or thought, except through Lanky? I had to wonder.

Finally got to prove my accuracy— still didn't count.

● DAY 145   I can't be sure why it is, but the realization has crept up on me that for the last month or so the Marine officers I see have been even more gentlemanly and warm toward me than they usually are. It's not that they were ever not nice, it's just that now they happen into the work tent to invite me to lunch, or drop by asking if I need a coffee, or offer to walk with me to my tent when it's dark. Sometimes, they'll just stop by my desk, settle in, and tell me about their day or their worries.

Maybe they just need a sympathetic female ear. Maybe I've been here long enough that people in general have gotten to know me well enough to be friendly. Maybe they know I've faced a hard breakup. But I've noticed that this change came significantly about once my own team made so clear their dislike of me. For that reason, I find the friendship of the Marines especially welcome and comforting.

Tonight, though, I was genuinely stunned when a Colonel, who I never truly had the chance to know very well but respected for his impressive rank, strode energetically into the tent and told Lanky he required my assistance on a matter. Lanky smoothed down his uniform and rose to accompany us, and the Colonel, in a way that wasn't quite unkind but was clearly pointed, let him know that it was only my assistance he required. Lanky cleared his throat uncomfortably and sat back down, while the Colonel happily escorted me out.

"Please join me, *Doctor*," he said, emphasizing the word. Nobody ever called me Doctor here, and I wasn't sure I liked it. Here, I'm CC.

"Sir," I said, as we walked into the evening, "I'm confused, but whatever that was about back there, it wasn't necessary for you to have acted so kindly on my behalf."

"Ah, CC, but it was very necessary," he said, and caused me to wonder. Perhaps Lanky had actually said something unkind in one of his meetings with the command structure, and it provoked a certain protectiveness of me in response. A friendly "backlash" of sorts.

"Now, let's get some of the good chow, over on the British side," he put in cheerfully. He had a jeep, a wonderful luxury, and we drove. We chatted about the operational impact of cultural intelligence. We chatted about home. We had coffee. There was no other work he had for me to do.

● DAY 147 This was one of those rare days when something excit- ing, in a good way, happened! If not a chow hall, a store —a real store—opened on Leatherneck! I had been watching workers mill in and out of a large tent for weeks, and it was clear that *something* mysterious was going on. People speculated that it might be a store, but I didn't want to get my hopes up.

Today, the tent flaps opened, a banner went up above the entrance, and everyone was welcomed in. Just the concept of having a tent to go into that wasn't your sleeping tent or work tent was in itself exciting. The idea of being able to get wonderful things there, like cold sodas and famil- iar candy and American magazines, was almost overwhelming.

It's funny the childlike delight it's possible to experience about some things when it's been forever since you've seen them. I heard even the most grizzled of Marine sergeants exclaiming things like "Wow!" and "O my gosh! Lemon drops!" Grins broke out on faces that were carefully disciplined to scowl.

It was a huge store, not like the little one on Bastion, and it had cases of the *really* good energy drink that everyone loved, all the way from the United States. I was so giddy, I bought a whole cold case so everyone in line behind me would get a can before they sold out. Finally, the camp was beginning to reach more desirable levels of caffenation!

The store had aisles of the supplies one might need as well. It had patches in case you tore your uniform, and t-shirts in case yours were re- volting, and rifle slings in case yours broke. I passed a display of the Ma- rines' knives, the Ka-Bars they so loved.

I hefted one in my hand and tossed it. (I should have remembered to kick that habit after the Mojave.) It balanced beautifully. Grandma's switch- blade would always be my closest and last line of defense, but lately it seemed like a good idea to have a first one, as well, I thought. I presented it, along with my drink request, at the counter.

One of my many filmy leopard-print scarves had begun to wear, so I ripped it in strips and wrapped the knife's handle, both for reasons of fine fashion and for making its presence against the mottled tan of my pack a bit less obvious. I affixed it—hard to see but easy to draw—close on my gear. "Ooo-rah!" approved passing Marines, toasting me with their energy drinks.

The new Navy chaplain came out of the store and sat next to me on the cement wall I occupied. He liked what I had done with the drinks, and he bought a case to distribute after mine. "So, your Govie-issue outfit says you're intel, but are you a Sailor or a Marine?"

"Both at heart, Sir, but neither here."

"How 'bout you explain that over some chow?" he offered, so we went to lunch.

He told me his life's story, he talked to me about politics (not a favorite subject of mine), and he finally asked me, as a Chaplain, if anything had troubled me over the deployment. It was the first time someone had asked me that question, and I knew what I said to a Chaplain could go no further than him, so I told him I was still troubled by certain dreams.

I dreamt of the suicide bomber, and of the trap of the children with the snipers, and of the lost boy I somehow failed, and of the times my "protectors" had left me to defend myself alone, despite the fact that I had managed to do so.

"Oh, it's easy to explain why that last piece happened," he offered.

"Why?" I asked, welcoming the insight.

"You're not family, hon, not yet. They'll protect you when you're family. Go home and put on the uniform. Then come back, and you'll see the difference."

"I plan to," I told him, as I picked up my tray and thanked him.

● **DAY 151** Today marks the FET's first mission. We went out with a large group on a MEDCAP—an official and approved offering of general medical aid to the community. We helped set up large tents, and men came from the surrounding areas to be seen by dentists for toothaches, doctors for wounds, and whatever other little help our medical staff were able to provide in the field.

Of course, only men came to the open offering, so it was our task, as the FET, to visit local homes and find out what the needs of the women and smallest children might be. We took a female doctor with us. To some degree, it was shocking for FET members to see the chronic illness and malnourishment with which most women live, as it had been for me.

The ladies also saw, for the first time, the rage some men had against the idea of their wives receiving any help. Our feet were tired and our minds were sore with the experience by late afternoon. It was then that we finally came upon the Kuchi families I had visited earlier.

It seemed that in them the ladies spirits were lifted by some unspoken hope for Afghanistan and consolation for their fears, yet it was hard to say exactly why. It wasn't the colorful clothes of the women or the brightly decorated spaces. (They tried their best to make the inside of their new mud homes look like the inside of a traveler's tent.)

Far more striking was the easy laughter in and around the Kuchi homes. The friendly children giggled their exuberance. Women and men—husbands and wives—would share a joke and laugh wholeheartedly together.

I realized it had been a long time since I had heard genuine laughter in Afghanistan, and I was strangely moved. This was not laughter tinged by cruelty or mockery. With shared smiles and sparkling eyes, the gypsies' laughter reflected their simple delight in long years of companionship.

I strangely thought to myself that somehow in these gypsies, the outsiders to "proper" Pashtun society, I was witnessing the only truly happy marriages I would encounter. Why was this so striking to me? Why was I so touched by the sight of men and women content to be together? I would never have thought twice about it back home, but it stood out to me as an anomaly now.

I had slowly begun to absorb the normalcy of the culture around me, to the point where I accepted it without naming it. Thanks to the defining contrast of the Kuchi culture, I could name it now. To a great number of men, women were offensive. They were something perhaps necessary, but generally undesirable to be around.

Here, at least, in the remote parts of southern Afghanistan, women weren't "so treasured" that they were kept like princesses in their homes, which was how I was first taught to understand the gender segregation I would witness. As a rule, women weren't particularly liked. That's what made the gypsies' laughter so beautiful to me. Men and women *liked* one another.

Now all the experiences that gradually taught me of this offensiveness came rushing back. I remembered the first men I met—the ones who kept that brave unknown young boy—seeming to share a secret joke about their disgust at having to touch a woman. I remembered the day-to-day encounters that taught me how unworthy of simple, life-sustaining resources some village men thought their wives and daughters to be.

I remembered the extreme examples, from the sexual haven of the translator's tent, where the disgust at my presence was (understandably) tremendous, to the Mullah who tried so hard to convince me that he, unlike the "uneducated" men I would encounter, "actually liked women" and would be delighted to touch one.

The reason my job in this place was so challenging, in contrast with that of the FET which was charged exclusively with women's interaction, was that I was a woman, trying to help foster social and military relationships, more often than not, with men. However, this detriment also gave me a certain perspective that my male colleagues, however wiser it would have been to put them into the position, could not possess. I saw through the lens of experiences only I could have had.

I dare to observe that womanhood itself here warrants offense and distrust—much like the dog whose "dogness" warranted it earlier, much like this distrust warranted the outcome of my own trial in the U.S. rather than the actual matter of the case, much like this distrust results in the horrific violence and abuse that women have known in this cultural context, particularly, but not exclusively, under the Taliban.

Medical mission.

I understand now *that* women are offensive, but I have yet to understand why.

● **DAY 152** Oh! There's something I completely forgot to write about yesterday. It's not a professional concern, just one that I've always wondered about personally. I came here curious about local music.

When I'm trying to break the ice, or just have a light conversation when I'm vising a home, I often ask, "What kind of music do you like?" or "Could you teach me a song?" Shocking, at least to me, are the answers I usually receive.

"I don't listen to music."

"Well, what kind of music do you like to sing? Even just around the house?"

"I don't sing music."

"Okay, well, if you were putting your little baby to sleep, how would you do it? Would you sing him a lullaby?"

"No, no singing. He will sleep. That's pointless."

I was distressed. One of the most important windows through which to understand a culture, I always thought, was its artistic expression. How was I to make sense of a culture that seemed to give itself no music?

I knew there was Afghan music, heard in more populated parts of the country, but the rural culture here seemed to have no awareness of it or musical tradition of its own. Either that, or it was somehow so extremely secret they wouldn't mention it to me, but I couldn't imagine that to actually be the case. What was I to make of a culture that didn't sing?

I finally got a different answer yesterday and, as usual, it came from the Kuchi families.

"What kind of music do you like?"

"You know, the good kind! We wouldn't like bad music. What a question you ask!"

"What makes it good?"

Rolling their eyes, the ladies answered, "You can dance to it."

Excited, I asked, "Where do you hear it? Can you teach me any?"

"Silly girl, everyone knows it—just turn on the radio. Bollywood!!!" they exclaimed. And the ladies began demonstrating appropriate dance moves while the men got the radio working.

I couldn't wipe the grin off my face. When the FET caught up with me, they thought I had been in the sun too long. I wouldn't stop smiling.

● **DAY 154** Today is particularly worthy of a diary entry, as I visited a base housing some Italian forces in Farah province. I was thrilled to find out I was going. It was an area out of my geographical responsibility as a HTT member, but it was a new responsibility of mine as a member of FET. We were going to attend a meeting of local leadership as well as take the opportunity to engage some State Department personnel about women's issues in the region.

Table at Italian chow hall.

My heart stopped just a bit to see the Italian flag flying in Afghanistan. We had some time to kill between our helicopter landing and the start of the meetings. Logically, I made an immediate beeline for the Italian chow hall, certain that it must possess something far better than the offerings at Leatherneck. I never did eat there. I was stopped in my tracks by what I saw.

Amid the most primitive accommodations, there was one small table, beautifully set. It had a white tablecloth. The plates and cups were good china, and I wondered how they could have arrived in Afghanistan without breaking. The silverware was real. It was complete with a wine glass, crystal candlesticks, and a crystal vase. The simple flower in the vase was the only part of the setting that wasn't real.

Its presence struck me with all the sweetness and tragedy of a Puccini opera. The table was always kept, set with great care, waiting for the soldiers who would never return. I touched a hand to it with a kiss.

I went to the first meeting a bit distracted, and my Italian wasn't good enough to follow the translators too well, but things were fortunately uneventful. The second meeting, with the State Department, however, revealed something I found odd. I mentioned an idea that any program aimed at women's needs must, to some degree, take into account children's needs as well, as whatever resources a woman had were likely to go first to the children she was raising.

"Great," I was told, "then we really only need to worry about boys up to the age of six or seven. Girls we can start treating as women soon after."

The part about treating girls as having the same needs as women once they were well into their childhoods made perfect sense to me in this context. The part about boys, however, made no sense at all.

"Wait. What happens to boys after six or seven? They don't stop needing stuff."

"No, but they stop being the concern of their mothers, so they won't need women's resources."

"Huh? Why would a mother stop being concerned about a six-year-old, whether it was a boy or a girl?"

"Oh, it's not so much that the mother isn't 'concerned' in that sense, it's that the child is no longer her responsibility, and she has limited access to the child and therefore limited influence regarding his care."

I'm always amazed at how folks from all levels of the State Department manage to put things so, well, "diplomatically" when they make points that would send an average person's hair on end. My hair was on end.

"Why would a mother's access to her child suddenly become limited?"

"Well, at that point they're their fathers'. They spend time with the men of the village, and once they're able to do that, the men don't want them so much involved with their mothers anymore. The boys quickly learn to distance themselves from their mothers too. It's not a big deal. It's just the way the culture is here."

Once again, I want to understand this culture and its values on its own terms. On an emotional level that I keep out of my notes and only in my diary, however, this just rings a dissonant note. I suppose I can understand boys wanting to be "macho," but this was not the child's decision. Perhaps six-year-olds elsewhere don't want their mothers kissing them goodbye in front of the other kids in their kindergarten class. Still, I realize that plenty of other societies are warrior cultures, and a bonding to an intensely male identity is cultivated in boys at a very young age. I needed to respect this.

● DAY 157 A reporter from National Geographic Explorer arrived today. She was a sweet, blonde, gutsy girl who was hard not to think of as an immediate friend. Hearing about the FET, she threw on armor, shouldered a camera, and accompanied me and my interpreter on today's (very small) patrol. While her footage never aired, it became a beautiful moment to literally put a "lens" on our work.

We visited a Pashtun settlement with three households. Each one, having met us a few times previously, welcomed our new friend—a blonde American with a camera of all things—into their homes. They shared tea, talked to us about how their health was improving or needed improvement, and told us how the embroidery business, in which some of the teenage girls of the families had begun to engage, was progressing along.

The girls showed us their work. Their families were proud. I was overwhelmed.

These were people with hope for their own future and the future of their country. They put effort forward to ensure it. They were willing to welcome an unknown American—a blonde woman with her hair uncovered and her camera, which could show to the world the women of their household—without hesitation.

They bore us no hate, only kinship. Things had changed. Things *could* change. I saw it, through that kind reporters' lens, today.

I couldn't help but be reminded of the one other time a journalist had followed me on a patrol. It was such an unfulfilling experience, I disregarded mentioning it even in my diary, but I remember it now. She was horrified the whole time.

Her first statement, upon meeting me, was "It's so dusty, it's affecting my sinuses. I don't know how you people manage to be so dirty." She acted as if the dust was present because we were simply too uncouth to use a vacuum cleaner and an air purifier—or as if we, ourselves, didn't mind it.

I figured it was a bit of shock, much like what I experienced when I first arrived. I ignored the comment. When she followed me on patrol, however, I realized her attitude was real!

Need those crayons!

I was talking to the father of a large family. The conversation was going neither well nor poorly, but he was concerned about teaching his boys to read and write and having so little with which to do so. I realized that a gift of the school supplies the Marines kept in their vehicle—kits of crayons and pens and paper—might help things go better. I put a word in to the Sergeant next to me, and he passed the word along to the Marines back in the trucks.

A bit more time progressed and the conversation wasn't improving, so I asked the Sergeant how things were coming along with the supplies. He turned and bellowed helpfully:

"You get CC her f*cking crayons! I wanna see those crayons this f*cking instant!"

I loved my Marines—the way they could manage to fit the words "f*ck" and "crayons" in the same sentence, while actually expressing a thoughtful and generous intent. They arrived immediately and cheerfully with gifts for the children. The father was delighted.

Our reporter saw it differently. "I can't believe the offensive language you people use so carelessly. You demonstrate your ignorance and violence at every turn." I was hurt for the sake of the Marines.

They were doing whatever was necessary to help me and to help this family. Yes, the work here is gruff. Yes, the work here is dirty. That's how we were bringing about the change we witnessed so beautifully today.

● **DAY 158** Kilroy was here. I couldn't help myself. I never thought I would be the kind of person to engage in graffiti, but it seemed the only right and loyal thing to do.

We are waiting for a helicopter from Leatherneck to Lash. Who knows if or when it will come. There's a wooden table here. It seems that many bored Marines before me have spent time contributing art to the tabletop.

However, Kilroy wasn't there. Kilroy was a beloved figure to the troops in World War II. He was particularly loved by my Grandpa.

Now, having rethought Grandpa's role in the war, I've begun to understand the humor. Grandpa would draw Kilroy in mischievous places. He'd draw him in places he wasn't supposed to be, just to say an American had been there—like Kilroy—peeking over the wall. I drew him for Grandpa.

Shura

CHAPTER 19

NATO Soldiers as Objects

● DAY 160

We've made it to Lash for a meeting with the head of the UK-based cultural research program similar to HTT. The tiny body of troops here was apparently so happy with the information on humor, the larger organization hoped to pose another question. Their program does not deploy teams, as the US does, and the director shared that despite the expertise of the people who work in their department, they have been unable to adequately answer a question very frequently presented to them by deployed forces.

No one knew how to explain the apparently overt sexual propositioning of troops by Afghan men. (I had certainly noticed this in recent months.) They were not even sure if they were correctly interpreting the advances for what they seemed. What were, if anyone was willing to ask, the typical sexual practices of the Pashtun male population? Would I mind investigating the matter?

Excuse me? I had gotten so many somehow sex-related questions in the course of this deployment that I had to wonder if I was unconsciously projecting a Dr. Ruth-like persona. The establishment of the FET was a gender issue, and it brought up to me a great deal of confusion over gender relationships in Afghanistan.

That was a far cry, however, from overtly researching sexuality, let alone sexual practices. I thought of the well-shaven soldier and the disconcerted contractor, and I understood why the question was relevant. However, I also had to wonder too what research techniques I could employ for this tasking, especially as a female.

Nevertheless, I agreed to the project. I had certainly seen plenty of homosexual behavior among Afghan men, but aside from my concerns about grooming standards allowing beards, I didn't truly consider it a topic worth much official study. Apparently, it was more of an issue than I had thought if it was so prevalent that it affected Western interaction with the Afghan people to the point that high-level officials needed to answer the question.

How much of an issue was it to the Afghan people themselves, then? If this was an essential piece of culture, we did need to understand it better. After all, this war centers upon the people.

● **DAY 163**   Back at Leatherneck, I paged through my government-issued notebooks, sized just right for the pockets of my uniform, which had been my constant companions. Unlike my diary, which was a confidant, these were simply detailed recordings of each day's experiences. The first rule of my work was to meticulously record *every* experience with local and military culture, as you never knew what might prove valuable for later analysis.

The books bore the marks of everywhere they had accompanied me. The stains of spilled tea and the smell of cheap imported Turkish cigarettes, the dirt embedded from a quick tactical maneuver and the happy child's drawing on my paper with a brand new pen all came alive on the crumpled paper. I was swimming through a flood of memories, but I was searching for something very specific.

I needed to revisit the most overtly sex-related research experiences I had recorded. I had put some of the most uncomfortable ones out of my mind, simply because they were so unusual to me that I didn't really have a mental "file" in which to store them. Suddenly looking through the lens of sexuality, however, some of the most troubling unanswered questions I had struggled with throughout the deployment began to fit a plausible picture.

Unfortunately, as I sat alone on my bunk, my notes surrounding me in piles that began to reveal an organization, I was disturbed to see the picture that emerged. I remembered the lessons of intelligence analysis that I had learned in my early training. Two seemed the most important to me, and despite my discomfort, they screamed at me now.

One involved the analysis of competing hypotheses. It was a rule that ensured that the analysis you presented was the one that accounted for the greatest amount of evidence at hand. It made certain that, even unconsciously, you didn't settle on a hypothesis you "liked," or thought anyone else might like.

The other was more of a maxim than a rule, akin to ". . . and ye shall know the truth and the truth shall set you free . . ." emblazoned on the entry wall of a famous government space. It said that the sole job of an intelligence analyst was to "Speak truth to power." It meant that an analyst's job was to ignore consequence.

Ignore offense. Ignore politics. Ignore diplomacy. Ignore the influence of position or rank. Only find and tell the truth to the people who need to know it, whether or not they'd like to hear it. (It wasn't a job that made for popularity.)

Though I had many adventures (and frequent misadventures) as a collector of what was truly intelligence, be it classified or not, I still forever saw myself as an analyst.[8] I put back on my wire-rimmed glasses. Regardless of whether I liked what I was doing, after 120 days in Iraq and now 163 days in Afghanistan, I knew my job.

I leaped from my bunk and found our old corner of office space in the command tent. It had grown even smaller. The air conditioning, as was frequently the case, was out. It stayed out. The August temperature seemed beyond what I could endure. Able to do nothing else—even sleep had it been possible in the heat—I worked through the first night and soon found there were many more to go.

● **DAY 167** For the past five days, I moved from the computer only to shower, because the heat made any food seem incredibly unappetizing. I could be seen in my corner, wearing several identical versions of the coolest, thinnest military t-shirt I could find (pilfered from British supplies), with my hair caught up unglamorously in a bandana and circles under my eyes.

The generous Marine officers I have come to so appreciate occasionally smuggled me an energy drink, as I must have appeared to need one.

"Marine gasoline," they called it. It occurred to me that maybe I had followed in my Grandfather's footsteps—here I was, a "standby typist" after all.

No one but the Marines talked to me, most likely because I looked so engrossed! After all, I "liked writing papers," and I seemed to be writing one. I tried to research any previous academic findings on the topic of Pashtun sexuality whenever the internet connection at the camp worked. It continually depressed me to find more evidence that fit only the hypothesis I suspected.

This evening, I finished. The report is below. I am going to chow. I am finally going to bed.

Human Terrain Team (HTT) AF-6
Research Update and Findings

Pashtun Sexuality

BACKGROUND

The Human Terrain Team AF-6, assigned to the 2nd Marine Expeditionary Battalion and co-located with British forces in Lashkar Gah, has been requested by these forces to provide insight on Pashtun cultural traditions regarding male sexuality for reasons of enhanced baseline cultural understanding for improved interaction as well as any IO applicability.

METHODOLOGY

Because of the extremely sensitive nature of this investigation, traditional HTT techniques involving a directed research plan and series of interviews executed to generate, test, and confirm hypotheses are not feasible. Direct questioning of Pashtun male interviewees on the subject is further hindered by the female gender of the social scientist writing.

Instead, findings here will be based upon field observations and interview responses by Pashtun men which were revealing regarding the topic, although discovered through the lines of questioning of other investigations. As sexuality is an essential building block of all human interaction and culture, these incidences of insight have been abundant, even couched in other research goals.

Secondary interviewees who have had extensive relevant interaction have been debriefed regarding their experiences. These include public health officers and medics who have treated a number of Pashtun men for sexual conditions, and other service members involved, like HTT, in relationship-building and interpersonal interaction.

Extensive open-source journalistic and academic writings on the subject have been additionally consulted, some involving directly quoted answers from Pashtun interviewees. References are included for further examination.*

Key Observations

- A culturally-contrived homosexuality (significantly not termed as such by its practitioners) appears to affect a far greater population base then some researchers would argue is attributable to natural inclination.

- Some of its root causes lie in the severe segregation of women, the prohibitive cost of marriage within Pashtun tribal codes, and the depressed economic situation into which young Pashtun men are placed.

- Other root causes include a long-standing cultural tradition in which boys are appreciated for physical beauty and apprenticed to older men for their sexual initiation.† The fallout of this pattern of behavior over generations has a profound impact on Pashtun society and culture.

- Homosexuality is strictly prohibited in Islam, but cultural interpretations of Islamic teaching prevalent in Pashtun areas of southern Af-

---

* Nevertheless, this work remains an informal paper written in a deployed field environment with the limited open-source resources available and without access to an academic library. The Human Terrain System's Research Reachback Center (RRC) may have additional resources on the topic.

† While researchers may argue whether this can rightly be termed abusive when seen through a lens from within the culture, it is not arguable that it involves a great imbalance of power and/or authority to the disadvantage of the boy involved. (For information regarding the sexual exploitation of boys as part of Taliban and private militia indoctrination of pre-teen fighters, see the *New York Times* article by Craig Smith regarding "Warlords and Pedophilia" and the Reuters article "Afghan Boy Dancers Sexually Abused by Former Warlords"—both referenced in "Further Reading.")

ghanistan tacitly condone it in comparison to heterosexual relationships in several contexts.

- Pashtun men are freer with companionship, affection, emotional and artistic expression, and the trust bred of familiarity with other men. They often lack the experience of these aspects of life with women.

- This usurping of the female role may contribute to the alienation of women over generations, and their eventual relegation to extreme segregation and abuse.

FINDINGS

Military cultural awareness training for Afghanistan often emphasizes that the effeminate characteristics of male Pashtun interaction are to be considered "normal" and no indicator of a prevalence of homosexuality. This training is intended to prevent service members from reacting with typically western shock or aversion to such displays. However, slightly more in-depth research points to the presence of a culturally-dependent homosexuality appearing to affect a far greater population base then some researchers would argue is attributable to natural inclination. To dismiss the existence of this dynamic out of desire to avoid western discomfort is to risk failing to comprehend an essential social force underlying Pashtun culture—one with a variety of potential implications upon the efficacy and applicability of ISAF efforts and on the long-term future of Afghan society.

HTT is often approached for advice by US and British service members who report encounters with men displaying apparently homosexual tendencies. These service members are frequently confused in the interpretation of this behavior. The British newspaper article below may be written with an attempt at humor, yet the Marines quoted typify the reaction often seen in service members upon their initial encounters with Pashtun males. As HTT has observed with frequency while on patrols in Helmand and Kandahar provinces, these men are outwardly affectionate toward both one another and male ISAF members, are extremely gentle in their demeanor and touch, and have often taken great care in embellishing their personal appearance with fingernails dyed red, hair and beards hennaed in careful patterns, and eyes very occasionally subtly outlined.

The article titled "Startled Marines Find Afghan Men All Made Up to See Them," by Chris Stephen ran in the national newspaper *The Scotsman* on May 24, 2002. Not even in reference to the more heavily Pashtun southern areas of Afghanistan, it read:

> In Baghram, British Marines returning from an operation deep in the Afghan mountains spoke last night of an alarming new threat—being propositioned by swarms of gay local farmers. An Arbroath Marine, James Fletcher, said: 'They were more terrifying than the al-Qaeda. One bloke who had painted toenails was offering to paint ours. They go about hand in hand, mincing around the village.' While the Marines failed to find any al-Qaeda during the seven-day Operation Condor, they were propositioned by dozens of men in villages the troops were ordered to search.

Another interviewee in the article, a Marine in his 20's, stated, "It was hell . . . Every village we went into we got a group of men wearing make-up coming up, stroking our hair and cheeks and making kissing noises." Beyond reacting to the unusual sight of made-up men, which one can readily accept as a style unique to a different culture, these Marines appear to have no doubt that they were being sexually propositioned.

One of the primary and obvious causes of this cultural tendency toward sexual expression between males is Pashtun society's extremely limited access to women. Heterosexual relationships are only allowable within the bounds of marriage, and Pashtun honor demands that a man be able to demonstrate his ability to support a wife and family, as well as produce abundant wedding gifts for the bride and her parents, before he is allowed to marry. Therefore, given the economic situation of most young Pashtun men and the current state of employment and agriculture within the Pashtun regions of Afghanistan, marriage becomes a nearly unattainable possibility for many. A controversial *Los Angeles Times* article highlighted this issue and featured an interview with a young Afghan man whose situation was typical of this circumstance:

> In his 29 years, Mohammed Daud has seen the faces of perhaps 200 women. A few dozen were family members. The rest were glimpses stolen when he should not have been looking and the

women were caught without their face-shrouding burkas. "How can you fall in love with a girl if you can't see her face?" he asks.

Daud is unmarried and has sex only with men and boys. But he does not consider himself homosexual, at least not in the Western sense. "I like boys, but I like girls better," he says. "It's just that we can't see the women to see if they are beautiful. But we can see the boys, and so we can tell which of them is beautiful."*

Daud's insistence that his behavior should not label him as homosexual is the next important point in understanding the nature of this dynamic, and opens the doors to a complex interrelationship between Islam and its cultural interpretations. Even men who practice homosexuality exclusively are not labeled by themselves or their counterparts as homosexual. To identify as such is to admit an enormous sin in Islam—one punishable by death under the Taliban and one that would result in severe tribal and familial ostracization today.† However, it appears to be the label, not the action or the preference, that poses the greatest problem.

In the context of rural southern Afghanistan, the relationship between Islam (here defined as the teachings of Prophet Mohammed as expressed in the Koran) and what is believed about Islam by the local faithful can contain vast differences. This is in great part due to a barrier in language and education. Not generally able to understand Arabic, the language of the Koran which is not to be translated, the Muslim faithful of southern Afghanistan rely on the teaching and interpretation of local Mullahs to inform them of what the Koran says. The more rural the area, the far less likely it becomes that even the Mullah himself understands Arabic‡ and the more likely that what is taught is based upon local cultural tradi-

---

* Maura Reynolds, "Kandahar's Lightly Veiled Homosexual Habits" (*Los Angeles Times*, 3 April 2002).

† A punishment of death for individuals publicly labeled as homosexuals remains a possibility even now, outside of Taliban rule, if enforced by extremist family or tribe members. Familiar recent news highlighted the situation of the young Afghan actor who portrayed a victim of male-upon-male rape in the film *The Kite Runner*. He had to be removed from the country due to death threats.

‡ Reading and understanding Koranic Arabic are two very different things. Muslims around the world, regardless of their linguistic background, are educated in religious schools to be able to read and recite the Arabic of the Koran. That is, they are taught to recognize,

tion, independent of Islam itself. Homosexuality is strictly prohibited in Islam, but cultural interpretations of Islamic teaching prevalent in the area tacitly condone it in comparison to heterosexual relationships.

A typical expression, echoed by a number of authors and interviewees, is that homosexuality is indeed prohibited within Islam, warranting great shame and condemnation. However, homosexuality is then narrowly and specifically defined as the love of another man. Loving a man would

Nowhere to hide—Afghan plain.

therefore be unacceptable and a major sin within this cultural interpretation of Islam, but using another man for sexual gratification would be regarded as a foible*—undesirable but far preferable to sex with a ineligible woman, which in the context of Pashtun codes, would likely result

---

pronounce, and memorize the words in order. However, even this education does not teach students the meanings of the Arabic words they memorize. Students who do not natively speak Arabic, like those of Afghanistan, Pakistan, India, etc., remain dependent on teachers to interpret what is written for them, and these interpretations vary greatly dependent on the culture and agenda of the teachers.

* Here a religion that prioritizes love and the fair treatment of others is turned on its head and made to condemn love as the greater sin but to tolerate the selfish use and potential abuse of another person as a pecadillo.

in issues of revenge and honor killings. These killings are a Pashtun, not Islamic requirement, although the two tend to become inexorably bound in the minds of rural villagers.* Similarly, the social circumstance that has made women foreign and unavailable (excessive veiling, segregation, and exclusion from public life) is generally also attributed to Islam in Pashtun communities, but is in itself a cultural construct, passed and exaggerated through local tradition.

Another example of cultural misinterpretations of Islamic tenets, bent to support homosexuality over heterosexuality, comes from a U.S. Army medic completing a year-long tour in a rural area of Kandahar province.† She and her male colleagues were approached by a local gentleman seeking advice on how his wife could become pregnant. When it was explained to him what was necessary, he reacted with disgust and asked, "How could one feel desire to be with a woman, who God has made unclean, when one could be with a man, who is clean? Surely this must be wrong."

The religious basis for his statement lies in the Islamic regulation that women are ritually unclean for participation in prayer while on their monthly cycle. In the Koran, this tenet does not extend to imply that women are unclean or unapproachable otherwise. However, local cultural interpretations have created the passionately if erroneously held belief that women are physically undesirable. Interestingly, the Koran specifies a number of physical circumstances under which a man can be rendered ritually unclean, but none of these are extended to the belief that he is unclean or undesirable in general. Therefore, it seems possible that such interpretations of Islam are at some point picked and chosen to support already-held beliefs or tendencies.

Interestingly, the same medics treated an outbreak of gonorrhea among the local national interpreters on their camp. Approximately 12 of the nearly 20 young male interpreters present in the camp had contracted the disease, and most had done so anally. This is a merely anecdotal observation and far too small of a sample size to make any generalizations regard-

---

* From HTT interview dated 28 June 2009, regarding the relationship between Pashtunwali and Islam.

† From HTT interview dated 30 May 2009. Because of the nature of the details later revealed, the interviewee's name, specific location, and unit details are withheld to protect the anonymity of DoD employee patients. Further details are available from HTT upon request.

ing the actual prevalence of homosexual activity region-wide.* However, given the difficulty in procuring such data, it may serve as some indicator.†

Of greatest interest here, however, is the way the men reacted to the education offered them so as to avoid the disease in the future. They insisted that they could not have caught the disease sexually because they were not homosexuals—important evidence of the rejection of the label regardless of the actual activities in which a man engages. Instead, they concluded that it was the result of mixing green and black tea, which became a running joke throughout the camp. They also continued to return for treatment after re-contracting the condition, having not believed or heeded the instruction they received.

However, beyond the issues of poverty, segregation, and tacit cultural approval which apparently contribute to the prevalence of consensual sex among adult men, there seem to be darker underlying dynamics additionally at play. To begin illustrating these, HTT turns to a field experience in which a principle interviewee was a boy in his very early teens. His circumstance, combined with the nonverbal reaction of his adult male companions to the women interviewers present, was revealing regarding the social and cultural factors underlying the exchange. The following is quoted directly from HTT field notes of the incident:

> Upon arrival at Camp Leatherneck in Helmand province, HTT was initially limited in its ability to conduct research with foot patrols and therefore sought to engage Afghan truck drivers who came on to the base for general atmospheric information. For the

---

* Another medical professional's estimate of homosexual prevalence is featured in Reynolds' *Los Angeles Times* article (op. cit.). It reads:

  It's not only religious authorities who describe homosexual sex as common among the Pashtuns. Dr. Mohammed Nasem Zafar, a professor at Kandahar Medical College, estimates that about 50% of the city's male residents have sex with men or boys at some point in their lives. He says the prime age at which boys are attractive to men is from 12 to 16—before their beards grow in. The adolescents sometimes develop medical problems, which he sees in his practice, such as sexually transmitted diseases and sphincter incontinence. So far, the doctor said, AIDS does not seem to be a problem in Afghanistan, probably because the country is so isolated.

† These men were also openly observed to simultaneously share the same cots within their sleeping quarters, and did not appear to feel the need to hide or disguise this fact. Again, it appears to be only the label of homosexuality that causes them discomfort.

most part, such drivers are staunch allies who take enormous risks, as it is publicly evident that they assist American and Coalition Forces, and they frequently face reprisals from insurgent fighters. Also to be noted is the fact that truck drivers are highly cosmopolitan in comparison to most rural Afghan populations, as they have seen and traveled within many regions, to include western-influenced metropolitan areas. It should be anticipated that they would be therefore less likely to display local Pashtun resistance to the open and public presence of women.

On day one, HTT met only a group of four or five truck drivers, all of whom were from Helmand, living approximately 50 miles away from the camp. The most striking interviewee was a boy, about 12–14 years old, traveling with a group of older men. He spoke English beautifully, Dari beautifully, Pashto with apparent fluency, and when asked about other languages he knew, said he also spoke Urdu.* This was an absolutely brilliant child.

Asked why he was traveling with the other men, they identified him as their 'little mechanic' and said he could repair any problems they had on the road. This added greatly to the already very strong impression of the intelligence of this child.

The boy told HTT that he was traveling with his brother, an older truck driver, and that their truck had been hit by an insurgent rocket on their way in. (He was proud to point out the location of impact.) The referenced brother was not present [and could not later be located]. The boy also explained that while their time on the road could be shortened, they take a circuitous route to the FOB, lasting about 10 days, in an attempt to throw off or avoid Taliban attacks.

I was deeply impressed with the boy, yet experienced a sense of wariness from the men who combined looks of distaste among themselves with slightly-too-slow requisite politeness toward the two female HTT members present. They had no such apparent problem with the male Human Terrain Analyst or Team Leader.

---

* These linguistic abilities were confirmed by a fluent Dari speaker who was an HTT member at the time.

The latter of the two approached in a U.S. military uniform.* Therefore, the reaction of the interviewees appeared to be an issue regarding females, rather than an issue regarding Americans or the American Military. Nevertheless, I left the interview uplifted thinking that the future of Afghanistan was in the hands of brilliant, brave children like this.†

This incident was later re-examined in conversation with a group of American interviewees who together and individually spoke with many, many years experience working directly with the culture in-country.‡ They reminded me that one of the country's favorite sayings is "women are for children, boys are for pleasure." One of the interviewees shared stories of how groups of men, ie. shepherding parties, would always travel with one boy "for fun." Sadly, the talented young mechanic came immediately to mind. HTT produced a picture of him with the group of drivers, and the interviewees were quite confident that their worst suspicions were correct. One interviewee then told the story of a time he found a 14-year-old boy quite literally in the hands of a group of Afghan security guards under his command. He physically fought the guards to free the boy and drove him back to Kabul, hours away, returning him home to his family, from whom he had apparently been forcibly taken in order to travel with the guards.

While in many areas of southern Afghanistan such treatment of boys appears to be shrouded in some sense of secrecy, in Kandahar it constitutes an openly celebrated cultural tradition. Kandahar's long artistic and poetic tradition idolizes the pre-pubescent "beardless boy" as the icon of physical beauty. 19th-century British authors report their observations of Pashtun fighters singing poetic "odes of their longing for young boys."§

---

* Further regarding appearances for future reference, both female HTT members were well-covered in their attire, including long sleeves and pant legs. My own hair was covered with a scarf, while my female colleague's hair was worn long and down. This may or may not have affected matters, as the men present regarded us both with equal apparent distaste.
† From HTT personal field notes dated 5 May 2009.
‡ HTT interview dated 11 May 2009 conducted at Kandahar Airfield, with former USPI employees. Their previous experience included providing security for the building of the Ring Road over the many years of its construction, and working and living with locally-hired Afghan security details for highly extended periods.
§ Smith, Craig. Op cit.

The *Los Angeles Times* author cited earlier notes this tradition as alive and well in very recent literature:

> A popular poem by Syed Abdul Khaliq Agha, who died last year, notes Kandahar's special reputation. 'Kandahar has beautiful halekon,' the poem goes. They have black eyes and white cheeks.*

Further, even the newly re-emerging musical nightlife of southern Afghan cities idolizes pre-pubescent boy performers, whose star status lasts only as long as their voices remain immature. While these performers themselves may be quite innocent, the reputation of their availability to patrons of the establishments at which they perform is difficult to dispel.†

Known frequently as *halekon, ashna,* or *bacha bereesh,*‡ "beautiful" beardless boys are coveted, almost as possessions, by men of status and position for sexual relationships. Further, the more attractive or talented the boy is deemed, the more his presence elevates the status of his patron. In the article "Afghan Boy Dancers Sexually Abused by Former Warlords," various interviewees state the following:§

'Everyone tries to have the best, most handsome and good-looking boy,' said a former mujahideen commander, who declined to be named.

'Sometimes we gather and make our boys dance and whoever wins, his boy will be the best boy.' Former mujahideen commanders hold such parties in and around Pul-e Khumri about once a week.

'Having a boy has become a custom for us. Whoever wants to show off, should have a boy,' said Enayatullah, a 42-year-old landowner in Baghlan province.

A key feature of this relationship, slightly different from the homo-

---

* Reynolds, Maura. Op cit.

† Nick Meo, "The Boy Singers of Kabul" (*Moby Capital Updates*, 12 April 2005).

‡ The titles translate roughly as "gorgeous youths," "boy loves," and "boys without beards."

§ Anonymous, "Afghan Boy Dancers Sexually Abused by Former Warlords" (Reuters News Service, 18 Nov 2007). Interestingly, this article features the phenomenon as it takes place in several other areas of Afghanistan.

sexuality practiced by men with other grown men who have limited access to women addressed earlier, is its more coercive nature rooted in an imbalance of power (economic, rank-associated, status/age-associated, etc.) between the parties involved. According to one observer:

> An apparent distinction seems evident in this particular Kandahar variation . . . The dating and courtship appears more coercive, more opportunistic and seems to take advantage of younger guys who almost have no other choice than to accept the money or gifts from bigger and more powerful 'commanders' whose bit of authority is bestowed by their gang-member status, their guns and the shattered legal/police system.*

Even where the halekon tradition is not "celebrated" per se, it appears to underlie a number of Pashtun social structures, most notably the recruitment of very young "soldiers" by commanders of paramilitary groups. (This is so much true that even today, current law prohibits "beardless boys" living in Afghan military and police stations.†) This in turn fits under the traditional warrior ethos which defines the role of men within Pashtun culture. This dynamic played a major role in the functioning of the warlord culture that preceded the rise of the Taliban in Afghanistan.

By some accounts, the first incident that brought Mullah Omar and the Taliban to prominence in the eyes of the Pashtun people actually involved a dispute between two warlords over a particularly attractive halekon. This dispute took the pedophilia of the warlords to such an extreme that the locals themselves were repulsed and happy to embrace a force of reform. Tim Reid, in *The Times of London* writes:

---

* Dr. Richard Ammon, a clinical psychologist who maintains an internet database on worldwide homosexual culture at globalgayz.com, posted an interview containing this quotation. The article is titled "Interview with Michael Luongo on his return from 'gay Afghanistan'" and was posted in July of 2004. Micheal Luongo is in turn a recognized researcher of gay culture in non-western societies and author of the book *Gay Travels in the Muslim World*. Both the interview and the book are referenced in "Further Reading."

† Smith, Craig, op. cit. Also noted in the Wikipedia article at www.wikipedia.org/wiki/Gay_rights_in_Afghanistan and the Sodomy Laws Database, edited by Bob Summersgill, at www.sodomylaws.org/world/afghanistan/afnews009.htm.

In the summer of 1994, a few months before the Taliban took control of the city, two commanders confronted each other over a young boy whom they both wanted to sodomize. In the ensuing fight civilians were killed. Omar's group freed the boy and appeals began flooding in for Omar to help in other disputes. By November, Omar and his Taliban were Kandahar's new rulers. Despite the Taliban's disdain for women, and the bizarre penchant of many for eyeliner, Omar immediately suppressed homosexuality.*

Perhaps "repressed" homosexuality would be a more apt statement, as the cultural tendency has not disappeared. However, open displays of homosexuality, in which the label of homosexuality could not be denied, became publicly punishable by crude executions under the Taliban. Now, in the absence of this possibility, the underlying cultural traditions appear to be returning to visible life with greater freedom.

Now that Taliban rule is over in Mullah Omar's former southern stronghold, it is not only televisions, kites and razors which have begun to emerge. Visible again, too, are men with their 'ashna', or beloveds: young boys they have groomed for sex. Kandahar's Pashtuns have been notorious for their homosexuality for centuries, particularly their fondness for naive young boys. Before the Taliban arrived in 1994, the streets were filled with teenagers and their sugar daddies, flaunting their relationship. It is called the homosexual capital of south Asia. Such is the Pashtun obsession with sodomy—locals tell you that birds fly over the city using only one wing, the other covering their posterior—that the rape of young boys by warlords was one of the key factors in Mullah Omar mobilizing the Taliban.†

However, the Taliban should not be viewed as free of the culture and tradition of homosexuality of the Pashtun world of which it is a part. Writers have argued that even within the Taliban, the tradition of halekon and the isolation of boys from the influence of family while they are

---

* Tim Reid, "Kandahar Comes out of the Closet" (*The Times of London,* 12 January 2002).
† Ibid.

assumed into the identity of a fighting group in which they are also sexually objectified and abused, is precisely what occurred with prevalence behind the walls of the madrasas. The now-iconic *Los Angeles Times* article on the issue states:

> . . . many accuse the Taliban of hypocrisy on the issue of homosexuality. 'The Taliban had halekon, but they kept it secret," says one anti-Taliban commander, who is rumored to keep two halekon. 'They hid their halekon in their madrasas,' or religious schools.*

Whatever the source, there is frequently the risk that Pashtun boys will face a set of experiences that mold their beliefs regarding sexuality as adults in ways that are ultimately damaging, both to themselves and to Afghan society. It appears that this set of experiences becomes cyclical, affecting generations, and that the cycle has existed long enough to affect the underpinnings of Afghan culture itself.

From these findings, a model of this cycle might be ventured. It seems the cycle begins in isolation from the experience of women's companionship and the replacement of such companionship with men. Significantly, in the case of Taliban madrasas, many boys spend their formative years without even the influence of motherhood in their lives.† Women are foreign, and categorized by religious teachers as, at best, unclean or undesirable.‡ It is then probable that the male companionship that a boy has known takes a sinister turn, in the form of the expression of pedophilia from the men that surround him. Such abuse would most likely result in a sense of outrage or anger, but anger that can not possibly be directed at the only source of companionship and emotional support a boy knows, and on which he remains dependent. This anger may very well be then directed at the foreign object—women—resulting in the misogyny typical of Pashtun Islamism. Men and boys therefore remain the object of affection and security for these boys as they grow into men themselves, and the cycle is repeated.

---

* Reynolds, Maura, op. cit.

† This is often due to orphanhood or family separation because of refugee circumstances.

‡ At worst, women are categorized by such leaders as associated with evil—not unlike many Christian teachings over the years, emphasizing Eve's role in man's downfall.

The fallout from this cycle affects both genders, and could possibly be a part of what leads to violence against women and women's suppression in Pashtun culture. If women are no longer the source of companionship or sexual desire, they become increasingly and threateningly foreign. Two initial findings add to the cycle of male isolation from women. One, put forward by the Provincial Reconstruction Team in Farah Province,* who conducted regular round-table discussions with local women, is that boys, even when raised in the home, are separated from their mothers' care around the age of 7 and are considered the charge of their fathers.

Another, more complex phenomena, highlighted in the *Los Angeles Times* article as well as the Reuters article† and others, is that men who take on a halekon often attempt to integrate the boy into their families by marrying him to a daughter when the boy is no longer young enough to play the "beardless" role. This maintains the love relationship between the father and son-in-law which inevitably makes difficult the establishment of a normal relationship with the wife. The once-halekon becomes a father with his new wife, and then begins to seek a teenage boy with whom he can play the "bearded" role. The children born to this father inevitably register the nature of their mother's marginalized role. When to this is added the further isolation that occurs when boys are groomed for the halekon role by fighting groups or madrasas, it becomes almost unimaginable that boys would learn to form a normal and familiar attachment to a woman.‡

Talibs and halekon of fighters and other powerful men, when kept from the one universally nurturing experience of women—their moth-

---

* Taken from the non-published notes of the "Women's Engagement Binder" available at the PRT, and followed up upon by interview with former discussion leaders. USAID has taken leadership on the women's development front in Farah province, and can provide further information on request. The specific notes, titled "Women's Development Ideas," state:

> Though Islamic law stipulates rights to women, in the countryside it ranks behind customary/tribal law which is extremely harsh to women (think village honor code). Add Afghan superstitions and women take the brunt of it. A final influence is the community—for example once a boy reaches the age of 7, he is taken away from his mother and raised by his father. Mothers in law do not help in this process and are generally quite harsh to the younger ladies in a house.

† Reynolds, Maura. op cit. Anonymous author for Reuters, op. cit.

‡ This state of affairs perhaps made most evident in the words of the halekon themselves,

ers—are left with no way to relate to females whatsoever, and therefore no way to counter the negative labels assigned to women. While these men are excessively mild toward each other, the opposite side to the coin is a tendency to aggression toward women. HTT can again cite anecdotal but personal field experience which typified the way in which the behavior patterns of men, gentle toward one another, can turn quite opposite toward women, and the way these behaviors are imitated and transmitted to the next generation of men. The following took place on patrol in the Maywand district of Kandahar province:

Upon exiting the Mullah's compound, I was confronted with an irate neighbor—a man in middle-age, clean and apparently relatively wealthy in appearance . . . He expressed his horror that I, a woman, was present with the patrol. He would not make eye contact with me or shake my hand, but instead only referred to me with angry gestures. I maintained a respectful distance while he sat nearby to engage the men of the patrol.

When formally addressing the men, his demeanor changed. He shook hands with each, with every display of gentleness and respect. The traditional first handshake between Pashtun men grips only the first joints of the fingers, and he used this with each, along with much bowing. It was explained to him that I was present in order that men would not enter a compound where women might be seen, and he was significantly appeased . . .

After this conversation, as the group said their goodbyes and began to move away, the neighbor approached me and extended his hand. I took

---

featured in the article "Afghan Boy Dancers Sexually Abused by Former Warlords" cited in "Further Reading."

'I was only 14-years-old when a former Uzbek commander forced me to have sex with him,' said Shir Mohammad in Sar-e Pol province. 'Later, I quit my family and became his secretary. I have been with him for 10 years, I am now grown up, but he still loves me and I sleep with him.'

Ahmad Jawad, aged 17, has been with a wealthy landowner for the past two years.

'I am used to it. I love my lord. I love to dance and act like a woman and play with my owner,' he said.

Asked what he would do when he got older, he said: 'Once I grow up, I will be an owner and I will have my own boys.'

But Shir Mohammad, at 24, was already getting too old to be a dancing boy. 'I am grown up now and do not have the beauty of former years. So, I proposed to marry my lord's daughter and he has agreed to it.'

this to be an invitation to a handshake, offered now that he understood that I was there out of respect for the traditions of his culture rather than in an attempt to disrupt them. When I offered my hand, he took it in a crushing grip and with unexpected strength bent my wrist back into a painful joint lock.

I ultimately wrenched myself from his grip, and as I sought to rejoin my patrol, I was mobbed by the village boys, who I had previously showered with gifts of candy and school necessities, led by the neighbor's oldest son. This boy appeared to be approximately 11 years old. Grabbing my arm, he attempted to practice the same maneuver his father had demonstrated, to the delight and cheers of the younger boys.

The noise of the children caught the attention of our American interpreter, who returned and scolded them for their behavior. He attempted to shame them by asking "is this the way you would behave at home?" The oldest boy proudly answered that it was, indicating that his mother and sisters were treated with the same violence and disdain. While the encounter with the father hurt my wrist, the encounter with his sons broke my heart.*

In conclusion, due to both cultural restrictions and generational cycles of certain experiences, Pashtun men are freer with companionship, affection, emotional expression, and the trust bred of familiarity with other men. They often lack the experience of these aspects of life with women. This usurping of the female role may contribute to the alienation of women over generations, and their eventual relegation to extreme segregation and abuse. If ever the cycle of abuse is to be broken and the Pashtun culture heal itself from its wounds, which continue to fester in patterns of violence and conflict, the role of women as mothers and companions may be key.

---

* From HTT Personal Field Notes dated 15 May 2009.

For Further Reading

Anonymous. "Afghan Boy Dancers Sexually Abused by Former Warlords." *Reuters News Service* 18 Nov 2007. www.reuters.com/article/newsOne/idUSISL18489 20071119?pageNumber=2&virtualBrandChannel=0>

Ammon, Dr. Richard. "Interview with Michael Luongo on his Return from 'Gay Afghanistan'." *Gay Afghanistan, After the Taliban: Homosexuality as Tradition.* Updated 2004. 29 July 2009. www.globalgayz.com

Baer, Brian James. "Kandahar: Closely watched Pashtuns—A Critique of Western Journalists' Reporting Bias About 'Gay Kandahar'." *Gay and Lesbian Review* March–April 2003.

Chibbaro, Lou. "New Afghan Rulers Better for Gays?" *The Washington Blade* 21 December 2001.

Foster, Peter. "Afghan Tribesman Faces Death for Wedding to Teenage Boy." *Sydney Morning Herald* 07 October 2007.

Luongo, Michael T. *Gay Travels in the Muslim World.* Binghamton, NY: Harrington Park Press, 13 June 2007.

Meo, Nick. "The Boy Singers of Kabul." *Moby Capital Updates* 12 April 2005.

Murray, Steven O. and Will Roscoe. *Islamic Homosexualities: Culture History and Literature.* New York, NY: NYU Press, 01 February 1997.

Reid, Tim. "Kandahar Comes out of the Closet." *The Times of London* 12 January 2002.

Reynolds, Maura. "Kandahar's Lightly Veiled Homosexual Habits." *The Los Angeles Times* 03 April 2002.

Smith, Craig. "Shhh . . . It's an Open Secret—Warlords and Pedophilia." *The New York Times* 21 February 2002.

Steven, Chris. "Startled Marines find Afghan Men all Made Up to See Them." *The Scotsman* 24 May 2002.

Summersgill, Bob, compiler. "Afghanistan Sodomy Laws." *The Sodomy Laws Database.* Updated 2008. 29 July 2009. <www.sodomylaws.org/world/afghanistan/afnews009.htm>

Various contributors. "Gay Rights in Afghanistan." *Wikipidia.org.* Updated 2008. 29 July 2009. <http://en.wikipedia.org/wiki/Gay_rights_in_Afghanistan#Sexual_Abuse>

CHAPTER 20

It Doesn't End There

● **DAY 169**

I submitted the report yesterday, and I am already overwhelmed by its reception. I have received congratulations on such revealing findings, and I am grateful but not particularly pleased. The report became a consuming and somewhat painful task, as a topic I first considered essentially "light" devolved into one revealing profound abuse.

The report is gone from my hands and delivered in a final form. Only now, after the work is completed, do I truly realize that the confusion I've had over so many issues in the course of this deployment can be significantly addressed by the incredibly unexpected topic I investigated. The reasons for the extreme devaluing of women and the humanitarian issues that result from it are easily understandable from these findings. However, it doesn't end there.

One might also see potential reasons for the prevalence of drug abuse, the avoidance of reality, and the utter unwillingness to improve one's situation along with the expectation that recompense is owed, tied to a profound sense of victimization. When a person's hope and trust is destroyed through the terrorizing experience of abuse, and they have no example around them to restore it, how can they help but be resigned to their own tragedy?

From the Mullah who tried so hard to show that he, unique among his neighbors, liked women, to the waiflike young man who threatened a suicide attack, to the elusive boy I failed to rescue, their actions can be seen to make sense in the context of this investigation. Like the songs that come to my mind before I realize how accurately they've captured a truth, I think this, one of my last reports, has done the same for my long-standing concerns.

Village scene.

● **DAY 175** My colleagues are now quite aware of my findings, and has it begun to haunt everything we perceive. I suspect we will never be able to see the actions of teenage boys in the same way again. How are we to separate their actions of violence toward us from our awareness of their own victimization, and the cycle which perpetuates both? Even now that I am back to other work, this theme remains prevalent.

Now that fall has begun, it is a concern of the British commander if the surrounding communities have adequate supplies for the winter. He wants to know their needs in enough time to request and receive such items as extra fuel and blankets. Everyone's nerves remain on edge, as the previous month, August, has seen the most casualties of the entire war for the Brits because of a combination of suicide attacks, roadside bombs, and combat deaths.

Still, we sat in the mission briefing imitating the "stiff upper lip" of our colleagues. The job of assessing community needs fell to HTT, along with the few sturdy soldiers with whom we usually patrolled. Slasher, however, was only a week from going home, and would not be allowed to go on any more patrols.

British forces, which I have noticed over the course of my deployment appeared substantially comprised of Irishmen, Scotsmen, Ghurkas, various Pacific Islanders, and other "outsiders" to the mainstream U.K. community, seemed to have enormous hearts. At our compound, nobody within two weeks of returning home was allowed to go outside the wire for two reasons.

First, based upon informal statistics, it seemed the most likely time for "mistakes" to happen because the soldiers were elated and distracted. Secondly, and more importantly, nobody could stand the tragedy of someone getting killed so close to their anticipated return. Instead, Slasher would be replaced by the gentlemanly soldier we teasingly called Action Man. Action Man would earn his nickname in another way on our patrol.

We pulled out of the compound at Lashkar Gah in an "armored" British Army jeep. When we were with American forces, we often traveled in vehicles known as MRAPS. I loved MRAPS. Everyone knew it was possible to take a direct hit from a roadside bomb or a rocket-propelled grenade in an MRAP and walk away, battered but alive. By contrast, British Army jeeps employed technology developed for street conflict in Northern Ireland. They were designed to resist small arms fire and not much else. Non-American forces, lacking American resources, have courage bordering on insanity to regularly patrol Afghanistan in vehicles like these.

Not far out of town, a local youth, perhaps 16 or 17 years old, pulled up dangerously close to our jeep on a motorcycle, yelling wildly and waving something in his hand. This could mean nothing good. The Taliban employs two tactics involving teenagers on motorcycles. One is to equip a teenager with a grenade or explosive vest and a mission to destroy the occupants of a military vehicle. A grenade lobbed at or into our flimsy jeep would be the end of all of us (the boy included). The Taliban does this frequently enough to make us extremely wary of teenagers on motorcycles who got too close.[9] The threat is very real.

However, the Taliban intermittently employs a tactic even more disturbing. Teenage boys are recruited to *act* as if they are on such a mission, just like the young man who threatened my patrol before. I was far too familiar with the phenomenon.

These boys are tasked to get too close to our vehicles on motorcycles and appear on the verge of attacking us with grenades or explosive vests. The hope is to get us to fire on the boys out of fear, in the belief we are defending our own lives. It put us at a stalemate.

If we failed to stop the teenager, and he was equipped to attack us, as the events of recent weeks would strongly indicate he was, we were all dead. However, if we were to fire on the teenager and he was unarmed, we would give the Taliban a weapon more powerful than a suicide bomber and a victory even greater than the small prize of our deaths.

The Taliban, as extremist groups frequently do, would make the most of the incident in the war of public perception. A campaign would be launched based on the terrible fact that Western forces shot and killed an unarmed child. Even worse, those words would be true—regardless if the act had been based on an entirely different perception.

Photos and videos of the death and the grieving family would back up the story, and no one, besides anyone who had been in the same situation, would ever understand the trap in which we had been placed. As we see so often, these incidents bring to bear the resources of the world's media which, out of rightful shock at the tragic loss of life, unwittingly supports the intention for which the Taliban sacrificed the brave and confused young man.

None of us in the jeep wanted to kill the teenager, and all of us wanted to live. Given my recent work, we all suspected the abuse that might have brought the youth to the wiliness to act either as a suicide attacker or a willing victim for slaughter, and we saw him too, like us, trapped in an incredibly unfortunate situation. Still, it was more likely that he actually held a grenade and was about to kill us all than it was that he was part of a public-relations suicide mission.

Action Man was our gunner. There was no turret, but he stood with his top half poked through a hole in the roof of the otherwise closed-in vehicle and took aim with his rifle. He had the best view of the situation, and everyone yelled to one another to understand what was going on. He gestured for the boy to stop and everyone who could called out to the boy in Pashtu and Dari, "Stay Back!" "Stay Back!"

The first two rounds loaded in Action Man's rifle were warning shots. He fired one round. It did no more than make noise and send a well-placed "poof" of yellow smoke above the boy's head. If there was any misunderstanding on the boy's part, it was erased. The message to back off was clearly sent, and the wildly fearless boy, with suicidal commitment, still stayed glued to our jeep.

If a situation was not going to end with someone shot, it almost never escalated to the point where the second warning round, the red one, was fired. We heard Action Man take the second shot. Then, in a simultaneous decision to try to preserve the life of the boy, we started yelling. "GO! GO! GO! GO! GO!"

Our only option, if not to shoot the boy, was to attempt to get out of his range. He had a motorized dirt bike well-suited to the sandy dunes we were crossing. We had an old jeep well-suited to the streets of Northern Ireland. Still, that day, our jeep had wings. Quite literally. We took to the air over and over as we crested the hills at high speed. Our jeep lacked even the modern convenience of seat-belts or restraints, so we grabbed at Action Man's legs, which now dangled above us, to insure he didn't fly out from the roof.

I am the wrong size for most military equipment, and I never could quite get my big helmet to fit. In one of the lurches of our jeep, it was knocked away as I grabbed for the dangling legs. In the next moment, we were flying again, and my bare head was thrown hard around the "armored" interior. I lost awareness for a little while, because I don't know how the chase progressed from there. However, we clearly outpaced the boy, and kept him alive despite the apparent wishes of the Taliban, because we eventually arrived at the location of our mission—a village on the other side of a minefield that required us to cross on foot.

We had averted two possible headlines at home. One could have read "Western Forces Kill Unarmed Afghan Child," and, because of its tragedy and shock value, would have been endlessly repeated. Another would have read "Five Americans and Brits Killed in Suicide Attack," and would have been mourned. Under no circumstances would a headline at home ever read "Ragged Group of Americans and Brits in Rickety Jeep Desperately

Attempt to Protect the Life of Afghan Youth, a Suspected Victim of Sexual Abuse, who Appeared Intent on Killing Them While They Proceeded on a Mission to Ensure the Village of Said Youth Had Adequate Winter Heat." However, it's not the things most of the world hears on the news but this kind of crazy, complex story that constitutes the day-to-day experience of the men and women whose job is this war.

I got out of the jeep and, because of my bashed head, struggled to keep my legs and to avoid vomiting. I composed myself and we crossed the minefield toward the nearby village on foot, led by a soldier wielding what looked like a metal detector meant for the beach. The villagers were kind and sad, and their story broke my heart. Almost to a person, every adult was missing limbs or hands or feet or eyes, and a few children were as well. Their injuries were evidence that they had actually attempted to work their land.

They had bought their homes and the surrounding land from a swindler, who promised them a safe place to live after the Taliban took over their village. What he had sold them were homes on a densely-mined field. They didn't realize this until they started to explore the land, but the swindler who took their money was nowhere to be found. Now they had nowhere else to go.

It was not their need for blankets and winter fuel that needed to be brought to the attention of the commander, though that was included in my report, but the tragedy of their story about the minefield. This is where HTT work really can make a difference, as military forces may never have understood this without sending someone to talk freely to the village. However, with this knowledge, the military may be able to do something truly helpful, in addition to providing the winter supplies they had assumed might be needed.

We turned to leave, so we could bring this information back to the British commander. Then we realized that the little mine detector that had led us into the field was now out of power, or "dead" for some other reason. There was no doubt that mines were thickly-placed, as attested to by the missing parts of the people surrounding us. Word was passed that the plan was simply for us to walk out, hoping that we stepped where we had before. (I smiled confidently as we waved goodbye, but I think I wore out the set of rosary beads in my pocket as we made our way back to our jeep.)

Gratefully, we returned to the compound without incident. Instead of eating or resting, I completed the report, as I felt it was urgent to get the full information to the commander. I turned it in, headed for my tent because I still felt sick from earlier in the day, and collapsed.

● **DAY 179** Leatherneck again. One last time. The chow hall has its grand opening today, and I made it!

As thrilled as I am, there are many who are more so than me. The excitement has reached a feverish pitch. We've all waited so long, we're going to make this a celebration worth having.

I walked in. I don't know where they could have come from, but there were balloons! Streamers fell from the ceiling. Happy flags waved.

There were cook stations just like I imagined, and each was serving their very best. There was fruit, all sorts of fruit, flown in especially for the occasion. The salad bar overflowed, and there were even additional tables set up with fancy restaurant deserts no one had seen for endless months.

We thought the mood could not be more jubilant, but then we saw, of all people, CNN's Anderson Cooper himself sit down at a table. We were a bit awed at the presence of such celebrity. He was coming to cover the work here, I suppose, and he just happened to arrive on "chow hall day."

Then, it occurred to us. He had been told of our great trials—the way we lived in utter deprivation and fought on. Now this was what he saw. Balloons and banners and chocolate-covered cream puffs. Couldn't we have waited just one more day?!

● **DAY 180** With just a bit of wistfulness and an enormous amount of gratitude, I returned safely from my final patrol today. I was thrilled that it took place from Camp Leatherneck to the Helmand villages and Kuchi settlements that I have come to know well. I wanted to say my goodbyes.

When I arrived at the first Kuchi household I had visited, and the last one I would see, the ladies took me aside with great urgency. "There is something we really need to tell you," they said in whispers, as they led me by the hand. I took a deep breath, because I thought I knew what was coming.

HTT is not a classified intelligence organization, but sometimes villagers will pass vital intelligence information to whatever Americans they can contact. When this happens to HTT, we pass the information along to the channels that handle such things. Usually, the information is something like "I am afraid because I believe my husband is building a bomb in the back shed," or "There are twenty fighters hidden over that hill. Don't go home that way!"

I took out my notebook and was prepared to listen. "You must be having man troubles, dear, and we think we know why." Completely taken by surprise, I laughed out loud. Then, welcoming the advice, I asked, "Why is that?"

"Because you really don't do enough about your looks. We don't mean this the wrong way, because you're actually not extremely bad-looking. As far as Americans go, you've got the most potential to be attractive. However, you really need to change a few things if you hope to get a man, dear."

"Okay, what should I do?"

"Well, first off, you need to stop wearing that drab uniform and put on some color! You need as much color as possible!"

"It is my job to wear these clothes here, but when I go home, I promise to wear bright colors."

"Very good. Now, your face is so plain. You don't have a single tattoo. Grandma here did ours, and she would be happy to do some for you too." Grandma looked up and smiled at me from under her tent of shawls. I knew Grandma well because I had often tried to get her medical aid. She suffered from some condition that resembled Parkinson's Disease—her hands shook constantly. She winked and raised her shaking hands to reveal a sewing needle and a pot of ink at the ready.

Despite Grandma's shaking hands, she really had done beautiful tattoos on the girls' faces and arms, but I suspected she did them years ago. A part of me was tempted to agree, just to have such a special souvenir. However, I couldn't see grandma keeping a steady hand today. "Your tattoos are gorgeous," I told Grandma and the girls, "and I wish I could have one, but just like the rule about my clothes, I am not allowed to have tattoos on my face."

"That's terrible. You should really get a new job," they told me.

"I will when I go home. Is there anything else I should do?"

"Yes. By all means, wear more rings. You only have one. You should definitely wear another on your thumb at the very least."

This I promised to do, and to this day I wear a silver ring from Afghanistan on my thumb, just to remind me of the real wisdom of the gypsies—the loving way in which they relate to one another—and the hope I will always bear for the fate of their whole country.

● **AFGHANISTAN + 1**   I am writing from a Dublin pub, a Guiness on one side, and something deep-fried and delicious on the other. I am wearing the clean clothes I just bought. They give no indication of where I might have come from.

I hope, in fact, my cute new Irish cap makes me fit in. Most likely, I look like the silly tourist that I am. The tourist I'm thrilled to be.

The fact that I find myself here, of all places, is as surreal as it sounds, but I am simply on a stopover, waiting for the "Freedom Bird" to continue its journey. Everyone dreams about the Freedom Bird. The way home.

Months away from a deployment ending, talk at lunch tables will turn to the Freedom Bird. The flight is the diametrical opposite of the trip with the cargo in the C-130 that brings us in.

"It's just like first class!" everyone says excitedly. "There are big seats, and flight attendants to serve you drinks. Maybe you might get wine with your meal—and even though it's airplane food, it's got to be ten times better than the chow hall—and you get fancy hot towels that smell like lemon to wash your hands!"

Each of these simple things sounded like unimaginable luxuries worth longing for. I remember my Freedom Bird out of Iraq, and because it was chartered by the FBI, it felt like international first class all the way. I couldn't help yearn with everyone else for the joy of the indulgence.

Once I boarded, though, I had an experience even sweeter. The seats were small and tight, and the rows were seven across. I was in the center seat, preparing myself for what promised to be a *very* long flight after all.

"Wow! Hi, Ma'am," said the two young infantrymen, just perhaps out of their teens, on either side of me. "What are *you* doing here?"

It had likely been a long time since either of them had sat next to a female. They told me about going home. They told me about Tennessee and Wisconsin. They told me about parents and little sisters and sweethearts who waited for them.

Their excited smiles stayed on their faces as they fell asleep. Their heads came to rest on my shoulders. The flight attendant finally came by and waved for me to choose a meal, to take one of the nice little hot washcloths.

I winked and gently shook my head. I was the perfect pillow. I wasn't moving.

Sitting here in Dublin, I think now with all affection about each soldier on my shoulder whose name I didn't know. I think with all affection about the people I knew who worked so hard for peace: the kind Afghan schoolteacher, the gypsies who danced and loved in spite of it all, the Pashtun family who shared their grain with others, and the gentle children who waved and smiled. All of them fought, and they won their small victories every day by what they did. I am going home now, but may God grant that they not be abandoned in that fight.

Difficult to forget.

CHAPTER **21**

Afghanistan, Againistan

● AFGHANISTAN + 3

I realize that my diary begins in a new way now, but it certainly doesn't end. As much as I might want to put it from my mind, there is no way that an experience like the one I just had ever finishes. I saw that, more vividly than I could have realized, today.

I wore a rose in my hair today for the first time in a year. I walked out in red and black lace and, to the applause of an audience, played my flamenco. I was in the U.S. I was myself. And yet somehow I was neither.

I can't really imagine who thought this was a good idea in terms of scheduling, but it reminded me of the Carmen I sang immediately after returning from Iraq. I am jet-lagged. I need sleep. But perhaps what I need most is my music.

Still, I had the strangest experience of being in two places at one time. I was playing. I was in my safest, happiest place. And I was terrified. I saw the crowd and I saw the high places and close walls and I wondered how anyone was safe.

I knew the fears I had weren't relevant here, but I also couldn't imagine *why* they weren't. Did anyone realize what an easy possibility violence would be? America and Afghanistan seemed inseparably crossed in my mind.

It is true that I was frightened, and yet my thought wasn't illogical. In fact, I am just coming to realize that my strange bit of involvement in this long war may only point to the fact that all of us, as Americans, are caught up in a battle for our own survival, which is inexorably linked to the people and culture of southern Afghanistan (among myriad other places).

I understand so clearly now that the prosperity and safety of those places means our own. In the same way, a festering wound of abuse and violence left unaddressed, like the one of which I became profoundly aware, can not but impact our security—as we already have so vividly been shown. Whether we are willing or conscious participants in this battle or not, the fact remains that it is, most definitely and unpleasantly, upon us.

I played. At intermission I shook with tears. I fixed my makeup, and I played again.

I couldn't imagine that I might be compelled to write in this diary, a diary that was solely a chronicle of war, tonight, in my own bed. It feels "right," though, to express and examine my thoughts. It's occurring to me that perhaps the reality of war never really, truly ever ends.

I will write less, perhaps. I imagine my need to do so will fade. But sometimes, just sometimes, the bit of the war that was mine—the work I did with and about the people—will still require my reflection, I am sure.

That's what goes here now. Not my daily life, not my daily thoughts. Just those, in the pages I have left, that bind me still to Afghanistan.

● **AFGHANISTAN + 7** My dog—my big, beautiful, fluffy Angelo —who I adored and missed so terribly while I was gone, passed away today. Even while I was so far away, he was my guard dog. He kept me and my Marines safe because he showed me how to treat his doggie cousins across the world.

No dog, there or anywhere, is half the dog he was, though. A gentle shepherd and a proud and true defender. I'll never get over him.

● **AFGHANISTAN + 28** I once traded my leopard print for a grey suit, and a grey suit for camouflage. It feels so good to trade my camouflage for leopard again. Fashion aside, I am returning to normal work in the few arenas in which I do well. So, in addition to resuming a recital tour schedule, I obtained my PI license.

PI work can usually keep me close to New Mexico, where I prefer to be, and I found recently that I possess the somewhat unique qualifications to obtain a full PI business license in the state. My Mom, possessing similar inclinations, soon joined the firm, as did a range of other unusually talented individuals.

The license requires a firearms qualification, and today I visited the range. With the reassuring kindness of one of the most amazing firearms instructors I know, I shot a perfect score on a tactical qual. I took a deep, calming breath and re-holstered my prized new Glock.

The comfort of the pistol at my side, the absence of which had caused me such terror, finally allowed me a realization. I was home. I was safe. I was whole.

● **AFGHANISTAN + 62** The State Department called today. That's almost a funny sentence to write. The business phone rang early, my Mom answered, and called out in her inimitable way, "Oh Chica, this very pleasant lady from the State Department would like to talk to you!"

The woman who called thanked me for my report. She asked if I would give permission for it to be included in the department's training curriculum for employees assigned to Afghanistan. I told her that the report was unclassified and not my property, but that of the U.S. government. Therefore, there was no reason she couldn't use it, and I was personally happy that it might be of some help to her program.

She asked if they might seek my advice or further research in the future, and I said I'd be happy to contribute how I could. Then I went back to my coffee, still wearing my fuzzy morning slippers. That was weird.

● **AFGHANISTAN + 68** This morning, my Mom, the phone in one hand, greeted me with "Oh, Chica. This gentleman from the Department of the Air Force would like to talk to you." The questions from him were almost the same.

I was certain, though, when I came into the office this afternoon, that my Mom was teasing me when she handed me two messages—one from the Australian Army and one from the Swedish government. I tend to laugh like a horse when I think something is really funny. I did so.

She looked at me with concern, offered me some tea, and then suggested I return the calls.

● **AFGHANISTAN + 90** Okay, clearly it's not just me who's still thinking about the abuse problem in Afghanistan. Besides the phone calls, I still find reactions to my work from military members in my inbox, and I'm not deployed anymore. Whenever I did extensive reports for HTT, I tended to include my email address in case a reader had further questions. I almost never got one.

Now, however, it appears that the report on Pashtun sexuality has been uploaded on a variety of government systems and is being widely distributed—further than HTT work typically reaches. The interesting thing is the fact that besides reaching whatever bigwigs have called, the report is also reaching individual troops on the ground.

It's their reactions that matter to me most. Most just write to ask me if they can have a copy of the report for themselves. Many write with simple relief that there is some recognition of the phenomenon they felt they had been witnessing. Usually, these service members ask me not to share their stories, because they feel that speaking openly of this phenomenon is taboo and against our efforts to show respect toward Afghan culture.

I do not believe the open revelation of this phenomenon is disrespectful to the noble Pashtun culture but to a practice that is a criminal plague in any culture or context. I also do not believe that sweeping uncomfortable information under a rug is conducive to our efforts to effectively engage with the situation at hand. Therefore, I appreciate the seriousness with which the government and military community has begun to examine and incorporate this information.

One soldier, however, informed me with particular vehemence that I had not described the problem in terms of nearly the prevalence and cruelty with which he's seen it to exist. I thought of my work as rather extreme and explicit, so I can't imagine what he means. I'm not sure I want to know.

Still, I wrote to ask him to explain. He went silent. Now, I really do wonder what he witnessed.

● **AFGHANISTAN + 163** "Snowmageddon," President Obama has called it. They say this is the largest snowfall DC has seen in well over 100 years. I write only because I am trapped in a motel room, and there truly isn't much else I can possibly do.

After I started getting questions about my research, my PI firm eventually expanded into a government consulting/contracting agency. That's how I ended up here. Now the TV is out, the phones are out, and the snow reaches past all but the very top of my first-floor window. I couldn't possibly open the door if I had to.

I have no food, and I can't get delivery. This is a terrifying thought to an Italian. What if I survived Iraq and Afghanistan just to have my last diary entry written in the motel room where I perished from starvation?

I'm sorry. I tend to get dramatic when I'm hungry. I also tend to joke when I'm troubled by something serious.

Here, I have nothing but time to think, and my mind returns endlessly to the abuse issue. At first, the subject of the sexual exploitation of children in southern Afghanistan may seem a somewhat obscure topic—tragic, but of significantly less importance to our security concerns than, say, the opium and arms trades that financially support the violence of extremist terror groups like al Qa'ida. At this point, though, crazy as it may sound, I'm beginning to think that this issue might be of equal if not greater weight.

There's an aspect of the problem that my paper didn't address in any depth for its intended tactical and operational readership on the ground. However, now that the paper is unexpectedly being absorbed by numerous agencies on perhaps a strategic level, I think there are some additional global implications that need to be taken into account.

Foremost among these is the large-scale commercial aspect of the sex trade—particularly trafficking in women and children—that is prevalent throughout Southeast Asia and the lands surrounding, as well as in far too many countries closer to home. The pressures of Afghanistan's crumbled economy, coupled with some apparent acceptance of the use of children as sexual objects and women as expendable laborers, compel some families to do what seems unimaginable to us: sell off some of their unwanted or burdensome children to new "owners" or to traffickers. The 2010 Trafficking in Persons Report from the U.S. State Department manages to put this in sickeningly mild diplomatic language, stating that Afghan families "sometimes make cost-benefit analyses" regarding their "tradable family members."

Human trafficking and sexual exploitation presents a lucrative illicit trade comparable to that in arms or drugs, and just like these more well-known crimes, its proceeds very often ultimately fund terrorism. Unlike arms or drugs, a single prostitute can be sold to generate income over and over, and human trafficking offers simpler logistics to criminals, who can couch their operations in more easily explained guises. Well-established networks exist worldwide, typically originating in particularly disaster- or war-ridden areas where government control is weak, to funnel modern slaves into waiting and hungry markets. The U.S. is one of these markets, as is much of Asia, the Middle East, Europe, and Latin America.

Most sources consider human trafficking to be the third largest and fastest-growing source of criminal income worldwide, generating an estimated $9.5 billion per year. The 2011 State Department Trafficking in Persons Report states, "According to UNICEF, as many as two million children are subjected to prostitution in the global commercial sex trade." As this phenomenon is so easily hidden, it is reasonable to consider these estimates are conservative.

There is no way to think of the abuse issue in Afghanistan as small, or as irrelevant to our efforts against terrorism, or as lacking impact on a global scale. Sh*t. It's a much larger problem than I originally imagined.

● **AFGHANISTAN + 215**   Once again, the Pashtun Sexuality discussion is inescapable. It was revisited today when two friends from work (with too much time to browse the internet) pointed out that my investigation has found some unexpected resonance with the American media. My report has been referenced, but without mention of its authorship or origin, in both a PBS Documentary and a story for Fox News. Public awareness of the issue is certainly a good thing, and I am grateful to have my name left out!

The investigation by the PBS series *Frontline* titled "The Dancing Boys of Afghanistan" was conducted by the very brave and highly respected Afghan reporter Najibullah Quraishi. At the beginning of the show, it is explained that Quraishi was motivated to "investigate reports that Afghan boys are vulnerable to being sexually abused by powerful men who have brought back an ancient practice." My reaction to this television program is slightly mixed.

On one hand, it sheds desperately needed light on the phenomenon of child prostitution in Afghanistan, and it has begun to bring mainstream

American awareness to the issue. The exotic and unforgettable images of the boys, who were bought from their families specifically to work as entertainers and prostitutes, have enormous shock value. This ensures that Americans are likely to remember the story, which is critically necessary. On the other hand, the impact of this report is almost to make it seem that the only danger of exploitation that an Afghan child might face is to become a "Dancing Boy" of the *bacha bazi* tradition. In fact, while worthy of our awareness and action, this is a relatively rare phenomenon.

Far more common, and unaddressed, is the fate of the child who is simply abused in his home village, in the service the police, the military, or local warlords, or in the hands of the human traffickers to whom he is sold. This fate is far more mundane compared to the colorful yet horrific world of the Dancing Boys. Because of this, I fear it may fail to receive the full attention of the media, which may negatively impact the assistance that these children so desperately deserve.

If I had mixed feelings regarding the *Frontline* documentary, which was at least extremely thoughtfully produced and primarily concerned with the safety of Afghan children, I was somewhat shocked by the Fox News story, dated January 28, 2010. It focused on the sexual issues of Afghan men to almost the exclusion of any concern for abused children or the implications of the behavior reported for the treatment of women. While using my own words, it somehow framed the issue of concern as a "sexual identity crisis" among Afghan men.

Is this, I wonder—this tiny bit of salacious intrigue regarding foreign sexual "confusion"—all that can be understood of my work? Have I done anything at all to improve the tragic situation I witnessed? At the moment, it seems not.

Chopper. (Photo courtesy Department of Defense)

CHAPTER **22**

Farewell to Foreign Shores . . .

● AFGHANISTAN + 330

I've been meaning to write for two weeks now, and there's no way I've been able. Now, on a plane back to New Mexico, I comprehend something I glimpsed both in Iraq and Afghanistan, but I never truly owned. The Navy chaplain once told me as much.

Today I understand. I just finished my initiation as a Navy officer. I am overwhelmed with more emotion than I possibly could have imagined.

The training I went through wasn't nearly the miserable length of the boot camp to which enlisted Sailors are subjected or the ridiculously demanding ordeal that most officer candidates endure, but it was enough to teach us "DCO's." My company consisted of "direct commission officers," meaning that we had earned the credentials of officership in our fields elsewhere, and had both chosen and been selected to use them in service to the Navy. Therefore, happy to have us aboard, the Navy went easy on us in our training.

Still, these weeks have taught me what I needed to know. Just like in the movies, we were unexpectedly awoken our first day at three in the morning by a hugely intimidating, shouting instructor (with an impressively powerful bass-baritone) barking commands. We couldn't do a single thing he wanted correctly, earning us only louder shouting and a bit of physical punishment. (Try posing as if you're sitting in a chair without one, your head resting, as if pondering, on your fist, for a few minutes. That's the "thinking position," the one you use to consider what it is you might have done wrong.)

It wasn't really that bad, however, and somewhere, just beneath the instructor's "studly voice," as he referred to it himself, was a teasing smile —even affection for us obviously surprised and green newcomers. It was a game. We just needed to figure out exactly what the rules were.

The impossible demands continued. Our rooms, which we worked feverishly to make perfect, the hospital corners of our beds at precise 45-degree angles, were turned over, the mattresses flipped and our uniforms and belongings scattered through the halls, because we hadn't been precise enough.

We failed uniform inspections because our shoes were laced in the wrong direction. Quickly, our frustration taught us something. We tried to outsmart the instructor. If he was going to criticize our shoelaces, then we would get up earlier and made sure everyone checked everyone else's shoelaces.

If someone was particularly good at making perfect hospital corners, he made everyone else's while everyone else cleaned and prepared the rest of his things. We each found a specialty and helped one another. We were figuring out the game, we thought.

We began to like one another, to rely on one another—to depend on each person's generosity of spirit. "Sierra Company!" we began to exclaim in unison with pride when we were asked who we were.

The physical aspect (running miles at four in the morning along the beach, and doing more sit-ups and push-ups than we possibly thought we could) was grueling. There were bizarre demands on our clothing, our walking, our eating, and every other imaginable detail of our being. In addition, our day consisted of academic classes on which we would be tested and either pass or fail the course.

We were deprived of sleep and exhausted beyond our means to cope, but the classes were the most important part of our training. We stood rather than sat, so we could avoid falling asleep. We assigned each other particular portions to learn, and traded notes in the evening. We wouldn't let one another down.

So, the instructor tried to make us turn against each other. If one person made a simple mistake, we all endured the physical punishment—

usually an impossible number of push-ups—for it. We were smart, we thought. We had a policy among ourselves.

Whenever we were punished as a group for an individual's mistake, we never allowed ourselves to blame that person. It could just as well have been any of us, and no one wanted the blame to eventually fall upon them. The person who made the mistake got reassuring smiles, showing them that the push-ups weren't so bad.

We decided to be impossible to discourage in our cheerfulness. We wouldn't let anyone, particularly the instructor, see us down. When we were allowed three hours of sleep, and it was interrupted halfway through by a fire drill forcing us out of the building, we stood on the lawn in perfect formation. Then, as loud, happily, and off-key as we could manage, we burst into song.

"Anchors aweigh, my boys, anchors aweigh! Farewell to foreign shores we sail at break of day (day, day, day)!" We ran through every verse, then started it all over again. Our instructor could only shake his head. I wonder if he ever went home and laughed.

We had it together. We were passing our academics. We spun on our heels at just the right moments. We were pretty smug. "Walking tall and looking good, we ought to be in Hollywood!" we sang, as we marched in perfect time. Even our scary instructor finally allowed himself an open smile.

The silly demands and the marching and the shoelaces had nothing to do with anything. Being in the military didn't mean following mindless and arbitrary directions like those we were being given. That was just the game of training, and its lesson. Being in the military meant, more than anything else, being there for anyone who relied on you.

We were too smug, however. We asked for it. We found ourselves berated not by our own scary instructor but by a whole group of Navy Chief Petty Officers and Marine drill instructors (who managed some extraordinarily colorful language), apparently suddenly disgusted with us.

We were thrown in the "sand pit." In complete uniforms, we were made to lie in the surf. We were made to do push-ups to exhaustion, to the point of not being able to lift our faces from the sand. Then we were made to do more. The sand began to turn muddy, and the mud became unmanageable.

Then we were told to do a hundred sit-ups. We pulled each other out of the muck. We tried to do the sit-ups, and few of us could manage one. We tried until an idea struck us.

We started to link our arms. We started to brace our feet against one another. When the person next to you was in tears, you reassured them and you somehow found, where you had no idea it lay, the strength to pull them up with you—just for that one sit-up.

You were exhausted, and it was the person next to you who pulled you up. You lent strength where you could, and you had strength to rely on where you couldn't. We saw the surf rolling in toward us, the sun over the sea, and it was unspeakably beautiful. We did the hundred sit-ups.

"You have FIVE minutes. FIVE MINUTES, we heard screamed, until uniform inspection in DRESS WHITE." We were filthy. We ran, stumbling and falling, back to our bunks. We threw the muddiest of us in showers. We grabbed for uniform items.

In minutes we were clean and dressed. We fixed the lines of each other's collars. We checked each other's shoelaces. We had done this so many times, in our mind-spent exhaustion, we knew how to do it perfectly.

With thirty seconds to spare, we lined the halls, and even made sure each of our heels stood the same precise distance from the wall. We took a deep breath. We found ourselves at sudden still attention, perfect in our whites, with immense and inexpressible love in our eyes. We passed.

The love wasn't simply for the people there, we knew. We would likely never see each other again. The love was for everyone who would ever share the same reliance on one another, and who would ever rely on us. Our Shipmates, our Country.

"Shipmate," we called each other, hugging and slapping backs. "Shipmate," we couldn't say enough. We were Sailors, we were officers, and we, even the smallest among us, myself, had arms strong enough to bear anyone who needed to lean.

Our culture as a Navy, we insisted, is what made us Sailors. We all knew in the course of current wars, all our company would most likely become "sand Sailors," seeing service in the desert rather than on the sea we loved. Our work would bear little difference, really, to that of other services. Still, I knew my Sailor's soul belonged to the Navy, though the Marine Corps had come to own my heart as well.

In the meantime, during the course of the class, I heard the strangest whispers when we shouldn't have been talking. "Ssssst . . . Cardinalli, is this you?" someone asked, pointing to an online version of a newspaper in class. "Did you write about sex?"

"Cardinalli wrote about sex in the newspapers!," the confused telephone game passed around the room.

"What? Like an advice column?"

"Who knew?"

"No, look!" The story was in all the newspapers anyone checked, often on the front pages. Joel Brinkley, a Pulitzer-prize winning journalist, had interviewed me about my work, and now his article was syndicated.

I'll worry more about it after I get home and get some rest.

● **AFGHANISTAN + 333** My Shipmates were right. The article had gone everywhere. I think Mr. Brinkley, at least, got things right. I had been afraid, when I first heard the article had come out, that it was salacious, and made something of my work that it was not.

My Shipmates certainly made it sound that way, but they were just teasing me. They said they didn't know many "sex experts" and were delighted they knew me. The article was nothing like what they implied.

Unlike the previous article that had me so disheartened, Mr. Brinkley's primary concern was the abuse of children. He also actually called to interview me personally. He asked me what my real worries might be.

While Mr. Brinkley introduced a reference to the possible involvement of the Karzai family in the practice of child prostitution, which was news to me, he also allowed me to state the point I longed to make.

"There's no issue more horrifying and more deserving of our attention than this," I told him. "I'm continually haunted by what I saw." If this work has become public, I thought, I hope it might shock the general American public into a human rights concern about the issue.

The statement was a point I had not had the opportunity to make so strongly previously, even in my report itself. It was to say that my findings weren't an anthropological "oh, isn't it interesting that this is how things happen in another culture," but an actual condemnation of the abusive practices themselves.

I am finally encouraged in my hopes.

● **AFGHANISTAN + 335** I was up all last night obsessively reading internet posts, and I need to stop. They are upsetting me, and I'm not sure why the negative ones, which are the fewest, bother me the most. While Brinkley handled the subject matter with sensitivity, some responders have not.

The vast majority of the reaction was simply the public outrage one would expect regarding the large-scale sexual abuse of children. I am sincerely gratified and hopeful to see America react with the concern I anticipated. However, a few determined reactors have begun an ugly and angry internet battle.

Twisting the meaning and context of my findings, they accuse me of "Gay bashing." The purpose of my work was entirely *for* the protection of human rights and dignity, so I found it particularly distressing to see it somehow contrived to serve the opposite intent. I am also confused at how offensive such an argument must be to the community it purports to defend.

I can't imagine how someone would confuse Western adult Gay culture with abusive Afghan pedophilia. Much like the outrage I had at the South African contractor before I understood his concern, I am angry now. The accusation hurts more than I could have imagined.

I need time away from the computer so I can stop obsessively looking over the infuriating internet blogs. I must remind myself that most of the thousands of postings understand my findings and react with the moral concern I so wanted to see. Why am I so sensitive to the ones that misunderstand things? And how can they misunderstand things so severely?

● **AFGHANISTAN + 340** Okay, now this is getting funny. My few internet detractors posted what they have labeled "incriminating" video and photographic evidence of my incompetence in writing the report, therefore, by their logic, invalidating my findings. Apparently, I have an unacceptable tendency to play flamenco and sing opera. One never knows just when I might do it! However, it's possible to actually witness me in the act!

An internet search of my name reveals information about my music and concert dates. For obvious reasons, it would not reveal extensive information about my history of government employment or the specifics of my education. Dismay has erupted over the fact that I am a musician, which somehow makes my involvement in Afghanistan incomprehensible.

I must, therefore, clearly possess no education or experience relevant to the work I was assigned. I am sadly reminded of Lanky and Tex, who simply refused to comprehend that I might actually possess a Ph.D. and a relevant background, despite my appearance. There's not much difference here.

Then there's that photo from the Army newspaper, taken the day we dedicated the little chapel for the soldiers at Ramrod. It is particularly unflattering due to my closed eyes and open mouth (but at least I did remember my lipstick and earrings). I was singing Amazing Grace, and now all sorts of accusations surround that.

Perhaps I was employed by the Army only as a musician, not unlike a USO girl, and I wrote the report arbitrarily and unauthorized. Perhaps, because of the hymn, I was running around Afghanistan, proselytizing Christianity among the Muslim locals. (It is prohibited for U.S. personnel to do so.)

Whatever it might mean, it must be evidence I was doing something questionable! I suppose I can't do anything about what anyone thinks, so I've decided to give up so much worry. I'll continue to happily make my music, "scandalous" as it seems to be.

I'm back in DC, and I got an interesting if teasing question when I walked into work this morning. "Hey, Mata Hari, why do you do both?"

I swiped the donut of the gentleman who dared to address me so. Then I asked, "What do you mean?"

"Why *do* you perform and still do this other thing you do?"

I had to think. I supposed it originally arose out of some necessity, but why was I attracted to this work in addition to music as opposed to another field? I always believed that music, that art, was essential to our common humanity. It does something irreplaceable by both connecting us and elevating us to a place where we can love better, can treat each other better.

How is that possible or even remotely relevant, though, if anyone among us is simply too busy avoiding being brutalized or killed to be concerned about something like the elevating power of art? That, perhaps, is my answer to why the Pashtun women didn't sing. It makes sense now.

I can't do one without concern for the other, so I do both. I wasn't sure how to say that to my teasing colleagues. Tonight, though, I've realized that's how I explain it to myself.

● **AFGHANISTAN + 360** I wonder if maybe I've found the soldier who went silent on me—the one who told me he had a story to tell, then wouldn't share it. I located his screen name on a blog site today, reacting to the Brinkley article. I am going to try to reach out to him there. I wonder if he would possibly let me share his story as part of further research on the abuse topic.

CHAPTER 23

In From the Cold

● AFGHANISTAN + 371

H e is talking to me, but skittishly. His story, it turns out, was from his experience as a guard at the Guantanamo Bay prison facility. It's no wonder he was afraid to share. He sent me this:

> I would rather keep my actual name as disassociated from Guantanamo as possible. I've already been passed over for jobs because of my service there. It's not a place that is well understood, and after having fought for the last eight years to help people understand it better, I'm burnt out.[10]

It saddens me to see someone who argued for the human rights of children having to hide the fact of their service, and fight for those human rights he did. If not his personal emails to me, I can share what he already stated publically in an internet forum, reacting to my work.

> In GTMO, we had a kid who had been basically sold as a "tea boy" (sex slave) to a warlord in Afghanistan. When a SF [Special Forces] team rolled up on the compound, they caught the warlord's dudes making this kid fire an AK at US forces.
>
> Frankly, the US didn't know what to do with the kid. Send him back to the family that sold him into sex slavery? Send him

to Bagram where he'd undoubtedly be raped again? We ended up sending him to GTMO until we could sort something out.

We initially had him in units next to adult male prisoners. Not even mesh cages stopped these sick bastards from f*cking with the kid. We'd walk up to him curled under his bed, shaking and crying, as the f*ckstick detainees in the units around him would taunt/jerk off/spit at him. Eventually, we segregated him and a few others so that they could have a semi-normal existence learning to read and speak English.

When it was reported by the press that the kids were in GTMO, the entire international community was up in arms. Calling us war criminals, etc. I even had a few arguments with people . . . who would insist it was "moral" and "right" that we send the kid back to the family that knowingly sold him to a pedophile. Meanwhile, the kid was treated better by our guards than he had ever been treated by any of the adults over in Afghanistan.

Eventually, the international pressure was too much and we sent them back to their families. There were a LOT of pissed off folks in GTMO. Some of us had pushed to have families adopt them in the States so that they wouldn't have to go back to that nightmare. It wasn't politically expedient to do such a thing, I guess. I was personally disgusted with how we abandoned our principals, and it was one of the many reasons I left the military.[11]

My soldier is only an individual telling a single story from a single perspective, so he's not much of a "sample." However, his story is not of the sort that one can ignore without further investigation or can hear and go on without imagining its consequences and implications. What's scary is that his reporting runs quite consistently with the bits and pieces of information the public learned when the shocking news of the existence of children detainees in Guantanamo reached the media.

Just within the time frame in which the soldier dates his service, it appears three children were separated from the general population and appear to have been given the opportunity for "a semi-normal existence learning to read and speak English," as the soldier wrote. In a statement published on April 24, 2003, Lieutenant Colonel Barry Johnson attempted to explain the uniqueness of the situation.

They are in a secure environment free from the influences of older detainees. . . . They are receiving specialist mental health care, in recognition of the difficult circumstances that child combatants go through, and some basic education in terms of reading and writing.[12]

Clearly, this statement indicates a rather complete and sensitive understanding of the children's situation and needs, particularly regarding the "influences of older detainees" and the uniquely traumatizing circumstances of child combatants.

Chillingly, however, it was these inmates who were released in January 2004. Even the outspoken anti-Guantanamo researcher Andy Worthington confirms that the segregated children were the ones released, noting, "The three juveniles released in January 2004 were held separately from the adult population and given some educational and recreational opportunities."[13]

The issue of children in Guantanamo does not end with the three detainees—a significant number of children have been held in Guantanamo since these first inmates whose presence was revealed. There are well-documented cases of underage Afghan prisoners being held inappropriately. It seems too, however, that there existed cases of these children being held by necessity. What was the real nature of that necessity?

The Geneva Conventions and a number of internationally accepted agreements specify that children found participating in combat and detained must only face captivity in a case of extreme last resort. First off, my mind leaps to the circumstances that would lead a young Afghan boy to find himself in combat against US and coalition troops. My soldier's story did a good job of bringing to mind the life of a boy owned by a powerful local commander whose views landed the child on the anti-coalition side of the conflict. If not this, what else might constitute a case of extreme last resort?

Not every juvenile detainee will fit precisely the same abuse paradigm, but there is a thread of similarity in what brings young boys to the point of engaging in combat alongside the violent men who control them. Still, however, it almost seems as if the cruelty of a child soldier's original circumstances does not come into account when a media and political outcry rages against the children's separation from their families and homes. The wistful imagining of children longing for the day when they'll see their families again seems to capture the horrific depth of our misunderstanding.

Even Olara Otunnu, who as the UN Special Representative for the Rights of Children in War would be expected to offer a certain depth of insight on the topic, reacted to the Guantanamo issue with this unequivocal statement: 'Whatever the circumstances, children should be reunited with their families.'[14] Whatever the circumstances? The world's inability or unwillingness to see the situation of Afghan children in its true light seems to have made seemingly good intentions serve the worst ends!

Still, there were those who saw. There were clearly good people along the chain who wanted to do the right thing by those first boy prisoners— as challenging and uncharted as it was to sort out what the right thing would entail. Ultimately, though, the U.S. did not take that difficult path. It appears that we bowed to media and political perception rather than what was truly right for the children involved.

It leaves us to wonder and fear in how many other ways we might be doing this to various degrees, either willingly or unwittingly. I can only hope that as the reality of the scale of the abuse cycle that produces the young people whose hurt and damaged hearts serve the ends of terror in our world becomes apparent, we don't shy from the hard choices and the hard work. As we learn the truth, we must be compelled to do the right thing.

● **AFGHANISTAN + 429** Here we go again. Today I was faced with even more depth to the issue of child sexual exploitation in Afghanistan—this time because it actually involved American complicity and funding of the act! A reporter from the *Washington Examiner* called to interview me about a document found in the recent Wikileaks scandal. This evening, a west-coast talk radio show called to interview me about the same thing.

I needed to tell them each that I am horrified by the Wikileaks phenomenon. While some information can admittedly be unnecessarily over-classified, other information is classified, for instance, to preserve the identities of brave people who take grave risks to protect innocent lives. I am shocked at the carelessness of anyone who would risk the second in order to reveal the first.

Nevertheless, because of my research involving *bacha bazi*, they wanted to talk to me regarding a leaked revelation that DynCorp, the largest U.S. contractor in Afghanistan, had purchased the performance of a boy dancer. While I explained the social and cultural dynamic to the reporters—an opportunity for which I was again grateful in order to bring the human rights issue to further attention—I sincerely hoped that the purchase was out of cultural ignorance on the part of DynCorp. Given America's previous lack of understanding regarding the practice, I couldn't imagine how it could be otherwise.

However, I hope that this had made evident the fact that ignorance on this subject is something that we simply cannot afford. I've realized something more since I last wrote. While the role of the commercial sexual exploitation of children may present a factor in the funding of terrorism, the threat that this abuse constitutes to the security of Afghanistan and the U.S. is even more wide-reaching.

Ultimately, the real threat comes from the human experience of being terrorized which, once instituted, generally becomes bound to re-express itself unless the cycle can somehow be interrupted. Unfortunately, those with terrorist intent have capitalized on this cycle, so that the violence imparted to the children they abuse can be directed, not only to the next generation to experience the abuse, but to an identified outlet for violence—a Western enemy. Where this cycle of abuse has existed previously in Pashtun society—and perhaps even in the classical example of Greek society—it was used to create warriors out of boys.

The practice imbued its victims with a simultaneous sense of violation and rage, combined with a complex reliance on the warrior clan of men into which they were initiated. Rather than turn on their clan, their source of security, they found an outlet for their rage in the violence of war. As long as terrorists have this tool so readily at their disposal on a large-scale societal level, it will continue to produce generations of warriors for their causes.

● **AFGHANISTAN + 440**   It's actually taken this long, but I think I've finally truly settled back into real life and my real loves—the music career that brings me peace and is a prayer for peace in the world. Again I am the opera singer, the classical guitarist, the woman I was once so used to being. Oddly, only now I find myself a professor as well, and it's been two weeks since I started teaching.

Besides my Navy service as a Reserve Officer, I still feel a sense of further obligation to the military and federal community, so I agreed to teach when I was offered a position at American Military University in the Graduate Program of National Security and Intelligence Studies. My students are military members working on advanced degrees in their field. Most are doing so through the hardships of deployment. They have my utmost respect.

I am assigned a class on Intelligence Collections. I've been trying to teach something about the history of various collection disciplines, the relevant literature, and a bit of analytical technique. Nobody cares. Nobody signed up to learn that. It's become a losing battle.

Today, a student finally presented the real issue with an offer I couldn't refuse. "Dr. C., I promise. I'll do all the work you assigned, if you finally just answer our questions: What did you really do in Afghanistan? Why? Show us what real 'collection' means. And, I'm just too confounded to understand—what's sex got to do with it?"

I sat down to answer him. My goal was to answer my class, and perhaps to articulate the answer to my own self. I began the first few paragraphs of a lecture.

WARLORDS AND GOATHERDS:
THE ROLE OF CULTURE IN THE WAR ON TERROR

What was my job in Afghanistan? When I brief the capabilities and mission of HTT, I often put it this way: Other staff elements work to give the commander a perspective on the population. The purpose of HTT is to engage the population to such a degree that we are able to bring to the commander the perspective *of* the population. As a Social Scientist who was killed in Iraq said of the program, "At best, we try to represent the voice of the people in the commander's ear."

Why is this important? While both great violence and great heroism goes on in Afghanistan and Iraq, a war like the one on terror cannot be won by killing the enemy. It is most certainly not won in trenches by two groups lobbing bullets and bombs at each other, with one group ultimately proving superior at some point—although this is still the picture of war that many people back home carry with them.

For every one ideologically motivated insurgent we defeat with a bullet, two more will ultimately rise in his place if we do nothing to address the circumstances that made him somehow relevant or necessary to the people of his country, religion, and culture. For this reason, the way to victory begins with understanding the people themselves. The support of the people is what decides the winner in a counterinsurgency, and the war is one for hearts and minds.

Their needs, beliefs, and circumstances are either addressed by the insurgents or by the US and international community. If we can understand the people well enough to do a better job, the insurgents lose their base of support and ultimately fade into irrelevancy. That, and only that, constitutes victory.

I am not here to ignite discussion on foreign policy issues. Enough of that takes place on campuses already, and it belongs to the strategic realm of thinking. To answer your question, I can only bring you a taste of the tactical, operational, dusty boots-on-the-ground experience of integrating cultural perspective into the War on Terror, in the hope that it brings you a window on the people that you might not have had before.

Yes, many of you know that my most important work had to do with the roots of extremist violence lying somewhere in a dark pattern of abuse. These discoveries too, especially these, the darkest findings of a culture, are perhaps the most necessary. Without knowing the hidden issues, the uncomfortable issues, even our best attempts to address superficial issues will be ineffective and lead only to endless engagement without any true or final positive outcome. The hard truths are the ones we can least afford to ignore.

AFGHANISTAN + 500

An Epilogue

Today is, perhaps, the day I have waited for, though I believe I yet wait for so much more. Media reports worldwide announced that Afghanistan will sign an agreement with the United Nations "to stop the recruitment of children into its police forces and ban the common practice of boys being used as sex slaves by police and military commanders." This was not where it ended.

"With the agreement on an action plan to combat the problem, the government will for the first time officially acknowledge the problem of child sex slaves," the *London Times* reported. I found sudden tears. Finally. Finally, I thought, an official response.

The article announcing the agreement referred to my work as that of a "Pentagon consultant," who wrote "a report on Pashtun sexuality prepared for British and American troops in 2009." My work was part of this—a tiny part perhaps—but one that eventually helped make the situation impossible to ignore or deny.

I learned that even General Stanley McCrystal had been made aware of my findings, along with "NATO officials" unnamed. General McCrystal, it seems, was the first to take some action or offer high-level acknowledgement by issuing "an order in 2010 warning troops to be on the lookout for under-age recruits."

Though I knew my report had been widely distributed, until today, I never really knew if it resulted in any actual military or humanitarian impact on the ground back in Helmand and Kandahar. How high "up the chain" was my report ever read, I wondered, and did any resulting official action flow back down?

If my report went to the State Department, was there any effective diplomatic outcry that could come from there? If the report went to international NATO forces, did they seek action? Despite the media attention, it had seemed to me that the answer regarding any real impact was no.

Now there was something, at least something, that acknowledged the issue on a global scale. I'm not stupid, however. I understand that this is a signature on a bit of paper—a gesture and a hopeful promise. It can be nothing more.

I know better than most that the rule of Afghan law still lacks firm bearing or authority in the wild tribal lands of the south, fiercely though we all struggle to make it so. That struggle is resulting in some success. With the fighting we've endured and the lives we've lost and damaged, we've made safety in these regions—governance under Afghan rule rather than the reign of extremists and Taliban hold-outs—a real possibility.

We've made it, just almost, a place where laws banning the sexual slavery of children could be enforced and upheld. As I write, though, we are considering withdrawing our forces from what seems an endless war. It all feels like a gut-wrenching farce, the lives of brave fighters and good, kind Afghans, and innocent tortured children somehow the butt of the joke.

Is there a solution? It's extremely difficult to say how we might combat the dynamic of abuse, both for the sake of the human rights of children and for the sake of our own security. We can't forget, of course, that their security is also ours.

The first obvious issue is the fact that this cycle of abuse is generational. It therefore requires generational involvement if an intervention in the cycle is going to take place. At least one generation of children must grow up experiencing unviolated safety.

It would be ideal if these children knew continued caring contact with parents of both genders, so that women are not alien to boys nor men alien to girls. These children would then grow to adulthood lacking the compulsion to pass on any shattering hurt they had experienced. In the span of a single generation, the cycle of violence and terror can be broken.

How, then, might the safety of a generation be ensured? A significant part of the equation is the consistent enforcement of law and order by an effective force (not yet the Afghan Police and Army, who are currently the primary sex abusers cited by the U.N.). While the Taliban imposed its repressive laws with sheer unmitigated brutality, the post-Taliban Afghan justice system is not yet mature enough to enforce its own laws, especially in the most rural areas where abuses can be prevalent.

Next, the economic concerns that motivate families to sell children into sexual slavery must be addressed. However, I experienced firsthand the difficulty of motivating many citizens of southern Afghanistan to take personal charge of their income and the sustainment of their own families and communities. The Afghan government, most certainly, is not in the position to remedy the economic troubles of each individual village, and international forces and aid organizations cannot solve this problem long-term without the cooperation and participation of the Afghan people. Somehow, an attitudinal shift from the current and prevalent expectation of government dependence back to the ancient Pashtun ideals of personal strength, rugged independence, and individual responsibility to the community must be accomplished.

In addition, the safety of a generation must be ensured not only from widespread rape, but from the volatile external circumstances and strife that breed violence like rape. Still today, children grow up in villages where Taliban fighters come in the night leaving threatening letters, or arrive in the day and carry out their ghastly threats for all to see. Without a working security force, the Afghan villagers who sided with us and with the future of their country—who believed in a world where extremist violence had no place—will be the first to suffer the horrific retaliation of Taliban hold-outs, and their dream of peace will die with them. The lands will become again a breeding ground, quite literally, exclusively for terrorism.

Security, then, remains a necessity for the "ideal" generation to flourish. Again, however, this cannot yet possibly be accomplished by the Afghan Army or Police, the reality of whose functioning I came to understand so vividly while deployed. These forces will be capable, but not until they are spared the damage that currently renders them either addicts or abusers. Until, that is, a generation has passed.

The solution of seeing to the safety of an "ideal" generation is perhaps untenable, but it seems the only resolution to the cyclical violence bred by sexual abuse. The difficulty of solving the problem can be matched only by the danger of leaving it unsolved. The *London Times* included this photo

JN intervention. For all the writing I've done,
ore for me to say.

hildren
ne gyp-
fate of
of my

ttributed image.

A Parting Word

While I remain continually troubled for the of Afghanistan, I cling to the memory of sies' laughter, and its promise of hope. The hope I bear for the Afghanistan remains integrally linked to my wishes for the safet own country and that of the world. May we find a solution.

Notes

1. This is an Israeli martial art meant to provide an advantage to someone with a smaller and weaker frame.
2. It is thought that the Kuchi people are ethnically Pashtun and do not share the *Rom* bloodline of Gypsies elsewhere worldwide. However, even in apparent genetic and cultural isolation, their lifestyle and attitudes about their social place is similar to the *Rom* almost to the point of being exact.
3. The Liturgical Studies concentration had a bent toward art and culture and history, and it was there that I found my unexpected home. I also found friendships with professors and classmates whose unpretentiousness and brilliance I will admire for the rest of my life. To each, with happy remembrances of nights at Fiddler's Hearth and Bridget's, my love and thanks. I also wish to extend my deepest admiration and gratitude to Michael and Marianne O'Shaughnessy, whose support of the preservation of Penitente art and culture have made them an unforgettable part of my life and of the life and story of all New Mexicans.
4. I have never had any athletic talent or inclination whatsoever. I can't run fast. What I discovered about myself through running, however, is that I am blindly determined. In those days, I could run crazy distances because I kept putting one foot ahead of the other, despite my better judgment. After reading a book about Dean Karnazes, I completed the Marine Corps Marathon and the Marine Corps 10K together in a day for a 50K "ultra" run, and completed a second 50K the same week to help my office team from the FBI in a distance competition. Depressingly, we came in second.
5. To Swamp Ass, Dust Bunny, Popeye, Dirty Old Man, and those who can't be mentioned because they didn't have silly nicknames, my thanks.
6. After my parents' separation, Mom wasn't in a position to take charge of the care-giving situation—especially given my Grandmother's particular and inexplicable dislike of her. Her efforts to help were always rejected to the point that she assisted with stealth—always trying to send home-made meals and fresh sheets, but almost never being seen. I didn't have any siblings who could step in, so I needed to return home a find a solution.
7. Having given away my first watch, my options were limited to what the big PX in Kandahar carried. This watch was the only one small enough to fit, but it was clearly a "girlfriend gift," meant to be sent back home.
8. The HTT program, interestingly, is the first to literally close the "collector-analyst gap" for which the U.S. intelligence community has been criticized since the events of 9/11, by simply putting the same person in both roles. Despite its obvious problems, it is one

239

sure way of solving communication issues between the two! I find myself talking to myself all the time.

9. There were hardly any conceivable legitimate reasons for driving so close—within an arm's reach—to a military vehicle. Locals not involved with the Taliban, as well as anyone with common sense, knew not to approach military vehicles too closely, but instead to wait for them to stop or signal them to stop before attempting to talk with any of the occupants. American and allied forces even invested in massive public awareness campaigns to drive home this safety message.

10. Dated On September 20, 2010.

11. From a personal email with the author dated September 9, 2010. The same text was posted on an internet forum thread titled "Afghan Pedophilia Story" at the website mixedmartialarts.com on September 2, 2010.

12. Oliver Burkeman,"Children Held at Guantanamo Bay," The Guardian, April 24 2003

13. http://www.andyworthington.co.uk/2008/11/22/the-pentagon-cant-count-22-juveniles-held-at-guantanamo/

14. http://news.bbc.co.uk/2/hi/americas/2978661.stm